Senior Editors Elizabeth Dowsett, Tori Kosara
Editorial Assistant Lauren Nesworthy
Senior Designer and Brand Manager Rob Perry
Pre-Production Producer Siu Yin Chan
Senior Producer Alex Bell
Managing Editor Sadie Smith
Managing Art Editor Ron Stobbart
Publisher Julie Ferris
Art Director Lisa Lanzarini
Publishing Director Simon Beecroft

Edited for DK by Kate Berens and Kath Hill
Designed for DK by Simon Murrell and Mark Richards
Proofread for DK by Matt Collins

First published in Great Britain in 2016 by
Dorling Kindersley Limited
80 Strand, London WC2R 0RL
A Penguin Random House Company

10 9 8 7 6 5 4 3 2
003–290345–Apr/2016

A CIP catalogue record for this book
is available from the British Library.

ISBN: 978-0-24124-590-3

Printed in China

A WORLD OF IDEAS:
SEE ALL THERE IS TO KNOW
www.dk.com

CAPTAIN AMERICA ™

THE ULTIMATE GUIDE TO THE FIRST AVENGER

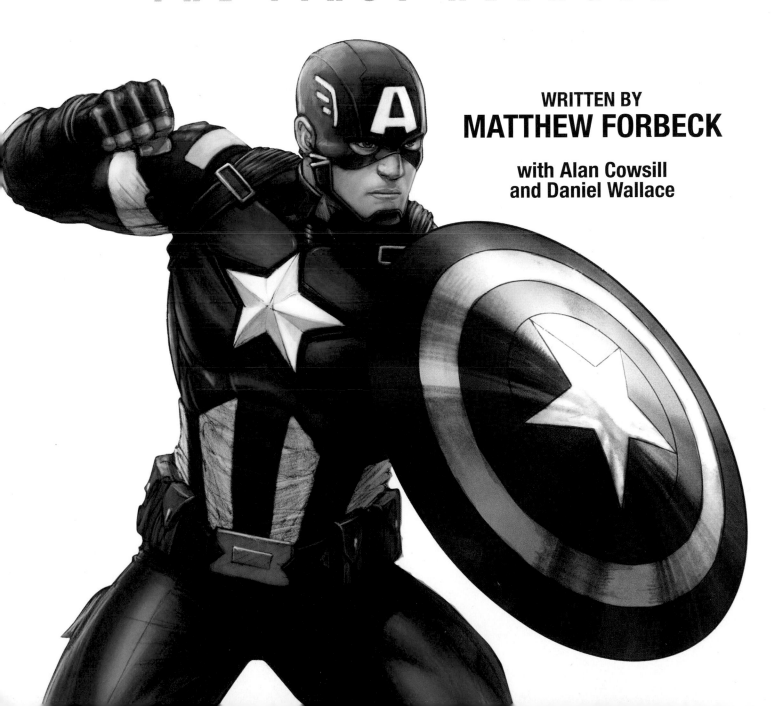

WRITTEN BY
MATTHEW FORBECK

with Alan Cowsill
and Daniel Wallace

CONTENTS

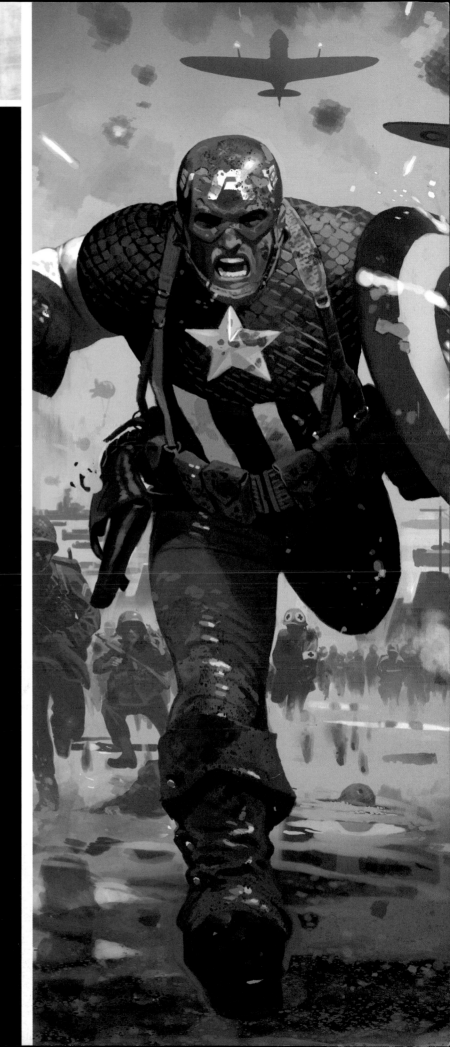

FOREWORD

He is, and will always be, the first Avenger!

Marvel's great red, white, and blue freedom fighter has captured the imagination, not only of Americans everywhere, but of liberty lovers throughout the world.

Created in 1940 by the titanically talented duo of Joe Simon and Jack Kirby as a symbol of freedom and resistance to the Nazi tyranny, Cap caught the imagination of comic-book readers everywhere.

Later, after Hitler's hordes had been crushed by the Allies, Cap's adventures were put on hold for a number of years. But I always had a place in my heart for the heroism and idealism of Steve Rogers and his shield-swinging alter ego, so in March, 1964, we brought him back again to continue his battle against evil of any type and any form.

Later, when we enthusiastically formed Marvel's great group of super heroes into a powerful evil-fighting team, it just seemed that the popular shield-wielding Cap was the logical choice to be the colorful leader of Marvel's mighty Avengers!

Now settle back and enjoy the saga of one of the greatest heroes of all—the freedom fighter and evil smasher known and admired throughout the world as the one and only—Captain America!

Excelsior!

Stan Lee

INTRODUCING
CAPTAIN AMERICA

It was 1940. Timely Comics needed a hit, and the US needed a hero.

The nation already had a slew of other costumed heroes, dating back to the pulp magazines that spawned the first comic books. But there was no national symbol, no all-American hero, wrapped in the Stars and Stripes, who had the bravery and brawn to fly over to Europe and break Hitler's jaw. That's where Captain America came in.

Created by Joe Simon and Jack Kirby, and published by Timely, which would become Marvel Comics, Cap and his pal Bucky stormed onto magazine racks at the end of 1940, a full year before the US entered World War II. The first issue ignited readers' imaginations and sold one million copies—a huge hit, even by modern standards.

Today, Captain America has been entertaining readers on and off for more than 75 years, with the famous shield wielded longest by the original Super-Soldier, Steve Rogers. Whether he's facing echoes of the real world—from war to politics, and social change—or battling his way across alien dimensions, Cap's remit hasn't changed since he first wore the costume. He still represents the power of the US, and shows us how it should—and perhaps can—live up to its loftiest values.

THE STORY OF CAPTAIN AMERICA

Created at the dawn of World War II, before the US became embroiled in the fighting, Captain America represented his nation's best ideals from the outset.

THE PUBLISHER

Publisher Martin Goodman had made a good business out of magazines, particularly the fiction-filled pulps of the 1930s. With the success of competitor's characters like Superman and Batman, Martin wanted to move into publishing comics. He contracted Funnies Inc. to provide him with material for his first comic—*Marvel Comics #1*—which featured the adventures of super-powered beings the Sub-Mariner and the Human Torch.

THE IDEA

Marvel Comics sold so well that Martin decided to start creating characters and comics in-house. Comic book writer and artist Joe Simon came to him with an idea he had had for a patriotic hero—the first to ever become involved in politics—who would symbolize America in the war brewing in Europe. He wore a costume colored like the US flag—complete with chainmail shirt and helmet—and carried a shield. He was given the name of Captain America.

THE CREATORS

Joe had recently partnered up with artist Jacob Kurtzberg, now known as Jack Kirby. Like Joe, Jack was from a Jewish family and his father worked as a tailor. Jack loved the concept of an American hero punching out Hitler. The artist insisted on drawing the entire first issue of *Captain America Comics* himself, even on a tight deadline.

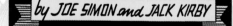

by JOE SIMON and JACK KIRBY

THE FIRST ISSUE

Joe came up with the plot and broke down each page with loose figures. Jack then stepped in and drew actual images. These were then inked up by Al Liederman. The trio managed to knock out the entire comic book in record time. *Captain America Comics* became a huge hit and this first issue sold one million copies.

THE STORY OF CAPTAIN AMERICA cont.

JOINING TIMELY

Captain America Comics did so well that Martin Goodman hired Joe Simon as Timely Comics' first editor. Joe set up the company's art department and hired his pal Jack Kirby as Timely Comics' first art director. They set to work on more comics featuring Captain America and a slew of other characters, laying the foundation for the Marvel Comics universe.

STAN LEE ARRIVES

In the early days of Timely, the comics line expanded rapidly. Martin Goodman hired many of his relatives to help out, like his wife Jean's uncle Robbie Solomon. Robbie soon brought Jean's 16-year-old cousin to the offices to see if Joe Simon could find him something to do, and Joe decided to hire him as an assistant. His name was Stanley Lieber.

CAPTAIN AMERICA FOILS the TRAITOR'S REVENGE

By Stan Lee

STAN'S FIRST STORY

To qualify for second-class mailing rates—a cheaper way to mail out copies to individual subscribers—comic book titles had to have at least two pages of prose in them. When Joe needed one for *Captain America Comics* #3, he decided to let young Stanley Lieber take a crack at it. "Captain America Foils the Traitor's Revenge" was the boy's first piece of published writing, and he used a pen name for it: Stan Lee.

"I'm sorry, Haines, but there is no place in this army camp for the likes of you. You have lied, cheated, spied, and stolen. Your conduct is no longer tolerable and I'm giving you a dishonorable discharge. Now get out!"

Private Steve Rogers, doing sentry duty nearby, was watching the scene interestedly. He had never seen Colonel Stevens so angry; and Lou Haines, too, was threateningly mad. The muscular giant shook his enormous fist at the Colonel

the camp gates, muttering insults under his breath.

Suddenly Haines felt a strong hand grasp his arm. He looked around into the flashing eyes of Steve Rogers! "I wouldn't act like that if I were you," murmured Steve, softly, "you were insulting a man in the uniform of the United States Army! Here are the camp gates; now beat it!"

Haines left, but there was a look of hate in his eyes which Steve could not help but notice!

"don't you EVER lose a game? I've forgotten what it feels like to win."

Steve smiled cheerfully. "I'll tell you what, kid: suppose you borrow a book on 'how to play checkers' and read it. That'll give me a chance to get some shut-eye. You don't know how tired it makes me to beat you all the time!"

Steve ducked just in time to dodge the pillow that Bucky threw at him. "Why, you little squirt" h...

Joe and Jack created the first 10 issues of *Captain America Comics* but then left the company. Casting about for a replacement, Martin Goodman chose Stan to become Timely's new editor, despite the fact he was still a teenager at the time. This was a position that Stan would hold for decades to come.

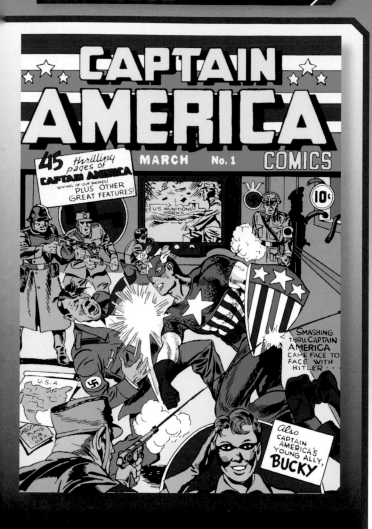

March 1941

COVER ARTISTS
Jack Kirby and Joe Simon

WRITERS
Joe Simon, Jack Kirby,
and Ed Herron

PENCILERS
Jack Kirby and Joe Simon

INKERS
Al Liederman, Joe Simon,
and Jack Kirby

LETTERER
Howard Ferguson

CAPTAIN AMERICA
COMICS #1

> *"We shall call you Captain America…"* PROFESSOR REINSTEIN

Main characters: Captain America; James "Bucky" Barnes; the Red Skull **Supporting characters:** Professor Reinstein; President Roosevelt; Agent X-13; Sando; Omar; Betsy Ross; Rathcone **Main locations:** Washington, D.C.; New York City; Camp Lehigh

BACKGROUND Marvel has always been ahead of the game. Even in its first incarnation, as Timely Comics, it was at the forefront of the newly emerging comic book medium. While other publishers had hinted at the rising tide of fascism in Europe, Timely—through the sheer creative brilliance of Joe Simon and Jack Kirby—became the first to tackle the threat head-on. Simon and Kirby's new hero, Captain America, not only fought the Nazis, but also punched Adolf Hitler smack in the face on the cover of his first issue. It was a brave decision. *Captain America Comics* #1 was created in late 1940, a whole year before the US would enter World War II, at a time when many Americans believed their country should avoid getting caught up in what was seen as a European conflict. Simon and Kirby thought differently. Although Cap didn't actually take on Hitler inside, the cover was a clear mission statement. Sales went through the roof, but it quickly became apparent that not everyone was a fan. After the issue was released at the end of 1940, a politically turbulent time with the US on the brink of war, the Timely office in New York was given police protection, ordered by the mayor of New York City. *Captain America Comics* #1 included the first appearance of the Red Skull, who would go on to become one of Marvel's greatest villains. This debut was later retconned to be that of an imposter, the "true" Red Skull not appearing until *Captain America Comics* #7.

THE STORY

Captain America's origin is revealed as he takes on Nazi spies, meets Bucky, and has his first confrontation with the Red Skull.

1

2

3

4

In 1941, undercover Nazi agents were committing acts of sabotage across the United States. President Roosevelt and the FBI hatched a plan in response, a secret project to create a "super-agent." Scientist Professor Reinstein gave a young, frail American patriot named Steve Rogers an injection—one that would transform him into a super-strong, super-intelligent hero. The Professor then decided he should be called Captain America **(1)**. Rogers was supposed to be the first of a new wave of heroes, but a member of the Gestapo had infiltrated the project and shot Reinstein, destroying his years of work on the Super-Soldier serum. A furious Rogers punched the spy, who staggered back into a bank of machinery and met a grisly death.

Captain America soon became a national hero. He gained a sidekick in Bucky Barnes **(2)**, when the regiment's teen mascot discovered Rogers was Captain America. The heroic duo investigated a stage act, Sando and Omar, who were able to predict attacks just before they occurred. Cap and Bucky found that Sando was actually a German agent named Von Krantz and was holding a reporter, Betsy Ross, prisoner. Cap managed to free the reporter and put a stop to the agent's attacks. Soon after, Cap and Bucky uncovered a Nazi agent trying to poison the soup in the Camp's mess.

Later they encountered Rathcone, another German agent, who had plans to take over the US. Rathcone sent assassins to kill various high-ranking military officials, using a chessboard to plan his moves **(3)**. When one of his agents killed Admiral Perkins at a lecture Cap and Bucky were attending, the duo investigated. Rathcone assassinated a general, then decided his next victims would be Cap and Bucky. Bucky was captured, but Cap soon tracked him down, making short work of the villain and his gang.

The Nazi threat was only just beginning. Soon Cap and Bucky encountered one of Hitler's deadliest agents, the Red Skull **(4)**, who seemed to be using a "death stare" to dispatch his enemies—including a US general. Bucky discovered the Red Skull's headquarters, and was captured and taken hostage. But Cap soon arrived to save the day. Although Cap and Bucky defeated his men, the Red Skull himself escaped. He then killed another general, but Cap arrived in time to save the general's wife, as she stumbled onto the murder scene. The Red Skull almost got the better of Cap during a vicious confrontation, before Cap smashed the villain's mask, revealing him to be the industrialist George Maxon. There was no "death stare"—the Red Skull would terrify his victims with his appearance and then inject them with a deadly poison. Unfortunately for Maxon, during the fight he rolled onto his own needle and killed himself. FBI men later found a letter from Hitler in Maxon's pocket, promising him a government post when the Germans conquered the United States. It seemed that the career of the Red Skull was over.

CAP'S WORLD

The bold letter A stands for "America" and always appears on Cap's forehead—it's one of the most famous features of his uniform.

The white star on Captain America's chest has always been a central element of his patriotic costume.

MASK

When Steve Rogers began his costumed career during World War II, he needed to keep his true identity secret, so he wore a mask, or cowl, that covered much of his head. The small wings on either side of the mask symbolize those of the American eagle.

Several versions of Captain America's uniform feature a fine mesh of overlapping, scale-like armor that adds protection while staying flexible.

SHIELD

Cap's suit is not fully bulletproof, so he uses his shield to deflect enemy gunfire. This iconic shield is used both for defense and offense. Cap can throw it with incredible precision, setting up a chain of ricochets that can knock out multiple enemies.

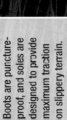

UTILITY BELT

Some versions of Cap's uniform feature pouches on his utility belt. These contain specialized gear for different types of missions. Typical items include first-aid kits, signal flares, climbing gear, survival rations, and tools for repairing machinery.

Boots are puncture-proof, and soles are designed to provide maximum traction on slippery terrain.

PROTECTION

Captain America's current uniform is made from military-grade materials such as Kevlar, Nomex, and titanium. Knives cannot cut it, and an inner layer of padding absorbs punches and heavy impacts. The uniform holds up even when sprayed with acids or blasted with jets of flame.

THE UNIFORM

The uniform worn by Captain America is both the protective garb of a soldier and the world-famous costume of a living legend. Its design has changed very little since the early days of World War II, when Steve Rogers first donned the symbolic red, white, and blue suit to fight the enemies of freedom. Though not fully bulletproof, it can safeguard against flying shrapnel and other hazards. Upgrades to its material over time have offered Cap some protection against electric shocks, fire, and extreme temperatures.

UNIFORMS ACROSS THE ERAS

Captain America's uniform is instantly recognizable—largely because its design has changed so little since World War II. There have been minor alterations to it over the years—marking significant events in Steve Rogers' life or indicating that a new hero has taken on the role.

The red, white, and blue colors have remained constant over the years, as have the stars and stripes on the uniform. These serve as strong reminders of Cap's nation of origin.

THE ORIGINAL • MARCH 1941

The US government used red, white, and blue to drape their champion in the colors of the American flag—serving as a positive symbol of the country's strong values and fighting spirit. This first uniform featured a detached headpiece that extended over Steve Rogers' eyes, concealing his identity, though it left the rest of his face uncovered. The triangular shield did not last long, and it was soon replaced by the familiar circular design.

THE CLASSIC • APRIL 1941

This look followed soon after Captain America's debut, and remained virtually unchanged for many decades. It incorporated a cowl that covered Rogers' ears and neck, and was made from tougher material that was more resistant to battle damage. After he was issued with this uniform, Cap received his nearly indestructible shield.

HERO REBORN · 1996

An immensely powerful psychic entity, known as Onslaught, transported Captain America and other heroes into an alternate dimension where their memories and histories were completely rewritten. The costume worn by this alternate version of Captain America featured a stylized eagle at the front of his cowl, instead of the letter A. The spread eagle resembled the one that was featured on the S.H.I.E.L.D. logo. Eventually, Steve Rogers broke free from this world and returned to reality.

THE ULTIMATE · 2002

The Captain America of the "Ultimate" universe—one of many alternate realities inhabited by different versions of familiar heroes—was more military-minded than his mainstream counterpart. Cap chose a uniform with laced-up combat boots and a more streamlined costumed silhouette that jettisoned the wings above the ears. The stars on each shoulder resemble military rank insignia. The breastplate was made from Vibranium and bulletproof Kevlar.

RETURN FROM DIMENSION Z · 2013

Steve Rogers spent 12 years in an alternate dimension, battling his old enemy Arnim Zola. When Rogers finally returned to the real world, it was as if no time had passed at all. He chose to put the experience behind him by suiting up as Captain America and returning to work for S.H.I.E.L.D. His new, short-sleeved costume featured additional armor on the shoulders, chest, and legs. Cap's cowl resembled a helmet, and was reinforced to withstand heavy impacts.

BUCKY BARNES · 2008

Captain America's wartime sidekick Bucky Barnes survived into the modern era as the brainwashed assassin the Winter Soldier. Steve Rogers helped his old friend shake off his mental programming and return to the side of heroism. When Rogers appeared to have died from a gunshot wound, Bucky Barnes became the new Captain America. Barnes felt unworthy of wearing his mentor's uniform and so he designed a new version in collaboration with Tony Stark. As a nod to his Winter Soldier training, Barnes wore a belt for carrying a pistol, combat knife, and other mission equipment. He continued to carry the shield.

SAM WILSON · 2014

As Falcon, Sam Wilson worked as Captain America's crime-fighting partner for many years. Rogers retired when the Super-Soldier serum in his body failed, and Wilson replaced him. Sam Wilson designed a new costume that incorporated red wings made from Vibranium, similar to those he used as the Falcon. The traditional Cap cowl was replaced by hi-tech goggles that enabled night-time and 360° vision.

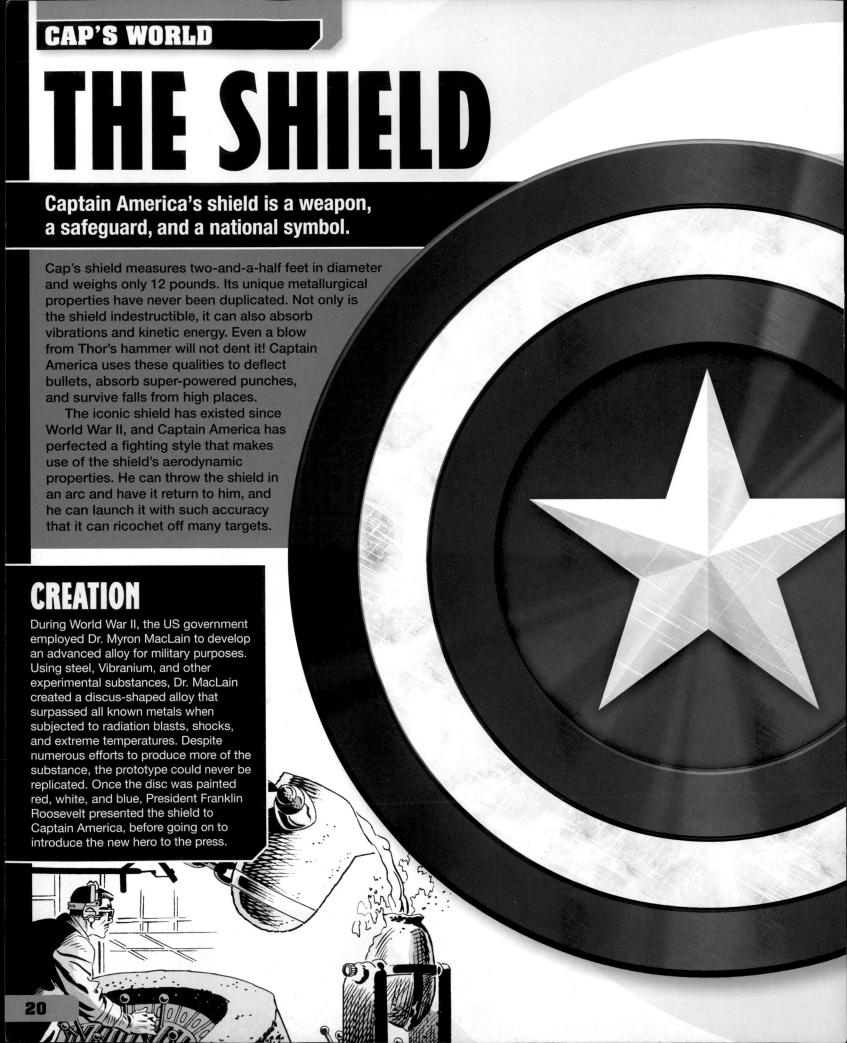

THE SHIELD

Captain America's shield is a weapon, a safeguard, and a national symbol.

Cap's shield measures two-and-a-half feet in diameter and weighs only 12 pounds. Its unique metallurgical properties have never been duplicated. Not only is the shield indestructible, it can also absorb vibrations and kinetic energy. Even a blow from Thor's hammer will not dent it! Captain America uses these qualities to deflect bullets, absorb super-powered punches, and survive falls from high places.

The iconic shield has existed since World War II, and Captain America has perfected a fighting style that makes use of the shield's aerodynamic properties. He can throw the shield in an arc and have it return to him, and he can launch it with such accuracy that it can ricochet off many targets.

CREATION

During World War II, the US government employed Dr. Myron MacLain to develop an advanced alloy for military purposes. Using steel, Vibranium, and other experimental substances, Dr. MacLain created a discus-shaped alloy that surpassed all known metals when subjected to radiation blasts, shocks, and extreme temperatures. Despite numerous efforts to produce more of the substance, the prototype could never be replicated. Once the disc was painted red, white, and blue, President Franklin Roosevelt presented the shield to Captain America, before going on to introduce the new hero to the press.

1 • FIRST EDITION

The US military issued this triangular, kite-shaped shield to Captain America, modeling it after the shield seen in the Great Seal of the United States. Made of steel, it could deflect bullets, but lacked the key aerodynamic properties that would allow Cap to throw it accurately. During World War II, Cap gifted this shield to King T'Chaka, the leader of the African nation of Wakanda, as a pledge of friendship.

2 • TRIANGULAR SUBSTITUTE

After giving his original shield to the Wakandan ruler, Captain America received a near-identical replacement—except for its stripes (the original had red and blue stripes). This shield was not used for long before the superior, circular design came into service. It did, however, remain with Cap's personal effects for years.

3 • INTO THE ROUND

It did not take long for the shield to adopt its familar discus shape. This shield featured a central white star on a blue circle, with red and white concentric rings surrounded by a blue ring. This blue-rimmed shield was used by Captain America during much of the 1940s. The shield's aerodynamic qualities meant that Cap could throw it at such an angle that it could return to him.

4 • "THE CAPTAIN"

Steve Rogers stepped down as Captain America when he became disillusioned with the government following a cover-up. Rogers' replacement, John Walker, received the circular shield, while Rogers became a solo hero known simply as "The Captain." Rogers wore a black costume and carried a black-striped shield, similar to those he had used as Cap. The first shield was made of Adamantium, and a second version was composed of pure Vibranium from Wakanda.

"The Captain" admires the first, plain shield made for him by Tony Stark.

The second shield was given to Rogers by the Black Panther of Wakanda.

5 • ENERGY SHIELD

For a time, Captain America used an energy-based shield designed by S.H.I.E.L.D. and issued to him by agent Sharon Carter. This device harnessed photonic energy into a disc-shaped shield that mimicked the properties of Vibranium. The shield's "flexibility matrix" meant it could change its shape into a staff or a knife. Controlled using specialized gloves, the shield could release photonic blasts at the enemy. However, there was a weakness, as Cap noted the shield's inability to ricochet off targets.

EXPANDING THE LEGACY

STEVE ROGERS

Every time Steve Rogers tried to volunteer for military service during World War II he was rejected for his sickly, scrawny body. But when Dr. Abraham Erskine chose him as the test subject for the government's Super-Soldier program, Rogers became a physically perfect human specimen. Dr. Erskine fell to a Nazi assassin, leaving Rogers as a one-of-a-kind symbol of his country's fighting spirit. In 1945, Cap seemingly perished in the explosion of Baron Zemo's drone airplane.

ISAIAH BRADLEY

The US Army's Super-Soldier program was intended to produce many perfect soldiers—not just Steve Rogers—but it officially ended following the death of Dr. Abraham Erskine. However, the government had secretly tried to copy Erskine's formula and tested it on 300 African-American soldiers. Only Isaiah Bradley survived the process. After escaping from German captivity following a failed mission, Bradley was imprisoned for stealing and wearing a Captain America uniform without permission.

WILLIAM NASLAND

The apparent death of Steve Rogers in 1945 left the United States government in a bind. Without a national symbol for American citizens to rally around, high-ranking officials felt that the country would suffer a loss of morale. President Harry S. Truman appointed William Nasland—the patriotic hero known as the Spirit of '76—as the new Captain America. Nasland died in 1946 while preventing the assassination of congressional candidate John F. Kennedy at the hands of an evil android, Adam II.

JEFFREY MACE

During World War II, New York *Daily Bugle* news reporter Jeffrey Mace was inspired by Captain America's example and became the costumed hero known as the Patriot. He served alongside other Super Heroes in the Liberty Legion, battling spies and saboteurs to help win the war. After William Nasland died in 1946, Mace took over as the third government appointee to wear the famous uniform. Like Nasland before him, Jeffrey Mace was a member of the All-Winners Squad. He left the role in 1949.

Steve Rogers became Captain America during World War II, and returned to the role several times. Yet there have been long stretches when Rogers could not serve as Cap—most notably when he was assumed dead—so other characters have stepped in to take on the mantle of Super-Soldier.

WILLIAM BURNSIDE

From boyhood, William Burnside idolized Captain America, and he devoted his life to the study of his hero following Cap's supposed death in 1945. During the 1950s, Burnside discovered the secret of the Super-Soldier formula and gave it to the US government—on the condition that he receive the treatment and become the new Captain America. Burnside even changed his name to Steve Rogers. In the end, however, he became so unhinged that he had to be placed in suspended animation at a government facility.

JOHN WALKER

After receiving superhuman abilities from the Power Broker, John Walker debuted as the Super-Patriot—announcing his intention to replace the "old-fashioned" Captain America as a modern American symbol. When Steve Rogers later resigned as Cap, the US government officially named Walker as his replacement. Though he did not last long in the role, Walker learned from Steve Rogers' example and stepped aside when Rogers chose to become Captain America once again.

BUCKY BARNES

Soviet scientists had turned Bucky Barnes—Cap's sidekick in World War II—into a brainwashed assassin called the Winter Soldier. Kept in suspended animation between missions, the Winter Soldier remained young into the modern era. Eventually, Captain America helped his former partner overcome his brainwashing. When Cap seemingly died, Bucky briefly took over the role. He wore a costume redesigned by genius billionaire and engineer Tony Stark (aka Iron Man), and carried a pistol and combat knife.

SAM WILSON

As the Falcon, Sam Wilson became Captain America's crime-fighting partner. Wilson wore a flying harness, designed by the Black Panther, which enabled him to soar at great speeds. He also worked with the new Captain America, Bucky Barnes, when Steve Rogers was believed to be dead. When Rogers returned, he found that the Super-Soldier serum was causing his body to age and named Sam Wilson as his successor. Wilson became the All-New Captain America.

23

CAPTAIN AMERICA

Steve Rogers was rejected from service in the US Army as physically unfit, but he was determined to fight for his country. So he volunteered to be the first subject of the Super-Soldier program, which transformed him into the perfect soldier. As Captain America, Steve became the living symbol of liberty.

ORIGINS

Steve Rogers was unable to qualify for US military service during World War II. He failed the physical examination to enter the armed forces because he was frail and sickly. Despite his rejection, Steve attempted to join the Army several times but never qualified. General Chester Phillips—the Army liaison to scientific projects—was impressed by Steve's determination. The General invited him to take part in Dr. Abraham Erskine's top-secret experimental program, Operation: Rebirth. The scientist's goal was to develop an army of enhanced human beings for the war effort.

Steve was the first person to receive a dose of the Super-Soldier serum— a formula capable of transforming human beings into Super-Soldiers. Steve was also imbued with Vita-Rays, which sped up the effect of the potion. Steve emerged from the test chamber in perfect physical condition.

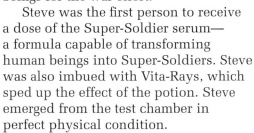

The Super-Soldier serum was administered in a secret lab in Washington, DC.

When the serum's success became apparent, a Nazi spy murdered Dr. Erskine. Steve accidentally killed the spy while attempting to stop him from escaping. But the spy's plan had worked. Dr. Erskine's secrets died with him, leaving Steve as the only member of the Super-Soldier army.

Steve then entered a rigorous training program. He became one of the greatest combatants and finest battlefield leaders in the world. He donned an American flag-themed costume and carried a triangular shield, becoming Captain America. Cap became a symbol of heroism and patriotism for the US, countering Nazi propaganda and challenging the Red Skull—the head of the Nazi's terrorist activities. With Cap's help, the US and its allies managed to turn the tide of the war and defeat the Nazis. American President Franklin D. Roosevelt later presented Cap with his iconic circular shield.

The Nazi's Red Skull plagued Captain America throughout World War II and for many years afterward. He pursues the power of a Cosmic Cube, which he plans to use to subjugate humanity.

"No one dies on my watch!" STEVE ROGERS

Captain America has served his country for more than 60 years. Despite his age, he is still in peak physical form. America's Super-Soldier continues to fight for freedom and justice.

Refusing to be merely a symbol for the United States, Cap fought alongside other heroes during World War II, including Sergeant Nick Fury and his Howling Commandos.

Cap's fire-retardant and water-resistant costume is made of Nomex, titanium, and Kevlar. His suit cannot be pierced by sharp objects.

Captain America's original costume had a separate helmet, but he had trouble keeping it on. A new costume was designed to integrate the helmet.

DATA FILE

FIRST APPEARANCE: *Captain America Comics* #1 (March 1941)

REAL NAME: Steven (Steve) Grant Rogers

AFFILIATIONS: Avengers, Invaders, S.H.I.E.L.D.

POWERS AND ABILITIES: Steve trained to become a master martial artist, shield-wielder, military tactician, and strategist. Additionally, he became an expert in weapons of all kinds, as well as a skilled acrobat. Although he does not technically have superhuman strength, he can lift weights of up to 1,200 pounds (545 kilograms).

Cap once had a system installed in his glove and shield to help him call it back, but the modifications imbalanced the shield, so he removed it.

Captain America carries an assortment of tools in his belt. What he carries in each pouch depends on what he thinks he will need to use on a particular mission.

AMERICA'S SUPER-SOLDIER

As America's one and only Super-Soldier, Captain America understands his importance as not only an agent for good, but also as a symbol of all that America can achieve. Although he is undoubtedly a true American patriot, he often makes it clear that he is subject to no administration nor government, but rather to the ideals upon which the US was founded. Cap stays above petty politics and those who would like to manipulate him and his imagery for their own gain. As he once told a US Army general who tried to misuse him, "I'm loyal to nothing, General—except the dream."

THE ORIGIN OF CAPTAIN AMERICA

America's greatest hero sprang from the efforts of scientists desperate to defeat the Nazis in World War II. They just needed to find the right man to do it—and his name was Steve Rogers.

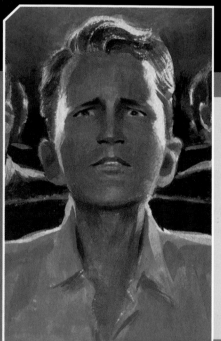

A MAN APART

Born on July 4, 1922 to Irish immigrant Joseph Rogers and his wife Sarah, Steve Rogers had always been a frail and scrawny youth. His father had been hard-pressed to find work during America's Great Depression and had turned to alcohol and abusing his wife. Joseph died when Steve was very young. Then, when he was still a teenager, Steve's mother passed away.

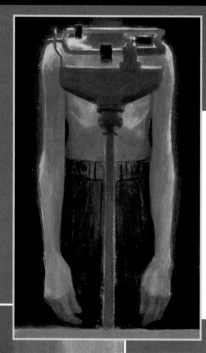

98-POUND WEAKLING

By 1940 Steve was a young man who wanted nothing more than to serve his country in the war he knew would draw in America. He tried to enlist several times but was always rejected for being too physically weak.

SOMETHING SPECIAL

One man, General Chester Phillips, spotted something in Steve he thought he could use for the top secret US military project, Operation: Rebirth.

A WILLING SUBJECT

General Phillips brought Steve to a top-secret laboratory and introduced him to Dr. Abraham Erskine, a German scientist who had defected to the United States. Abraham was the genius behind Operation: Rebirth, an effort to instantly grant even the weakest people their best physical potential by injecting a Super-Soldier serum.

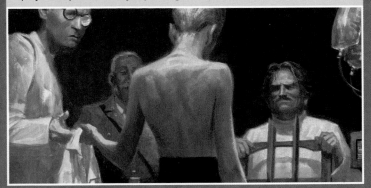

AN AMERICAN DREAM REALIZED

The Super-Soldier serum that Abraham had concocted worked perfectly. Steve instantly transformed from a frail weakling into one of the greatest athletes the world has ever seen. With the project such a success, Steve was supposed to be the first in an army of Super-Soldiers that the US would be able to field against the Axis powers in World War II.

FIRST AND LAST

Tragically, a Nazi spy sitting in the observation room above Abraham's lab wouldn't let that happen. He drew a pistol and shot through the glass at Abraham, killing him. Steve broke free from his chair and grabbed the Nazi, throwing him across the room. The spy landed on a transformer that electrocuted him.

The story continues...

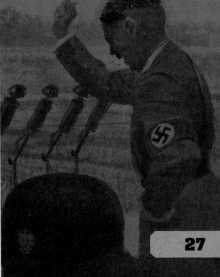

A NATIONAL SYMBOL

Abraham's secret formula for the Super-Soldier serum died with him. With no more such soldiers on the way, the US Army decided to turn Steve Rogers into Captain America. As Cap, Steve became a symbol of America and its willingness to fight for what was right. He helped steer the country toward joining the war against the Axis powers.

TRIUMPH OVER THE NAZIS

Once America entered the war, Captain America joined the fighting too. With the help of young James Buchanan Barnes—known to the world as Bucky—Cap helped the US take back Europe from the Nazis. Their greatest foe was Hitler's own icon of horror: the Red Skull.

HORRIFIC ENDING

In their last mission in World War II, Cap and Bucky tried to stop Nazi scientist Baron Heinrich Zemo's effort to send a drone plane filled with explosives toward England. Unfortunately, it was booby-trapped and blew up. Cap was jettisoned into the icy waters of the English Channel.

AN AMAZING RETURN

While out in their undersea craft, the group of Super Heroes known as the Avengers discovered Cap floating in a block of ice, his body preserved by the Super-Soldier serum. They thawed him out, brought him back to life, and he joined the Avengers in their adventures. Soon after, he became their leader.

A HERO IN ANY TIME

Whether battling Nazis in World War II or Super Villains in the modern day, Steve Rogers has always been more than a leader—more than a hero. He became a symbol of American ideals, of the best that all Americans could aspire to be. His legend only grew stronger over the years—the legend of Captain America!

FRIENDS AND FAMILY

Steve Rogers has a support network that extends far beyond the Super Hero community. Despite the fact that some of the most influential people in Captain America's life have passed away, the memories of their actions still serve as a source of heroic inspiration.

CAPTAIN STEVEN ROGERS

It is believed that Steve Rogers can trace his family history back to a soldier of the American Revolutionary War named Steven Rogers. This ancestor, who also went by the name of "Captain America," fought against the British around 1776. Rogers dressed in a red, white, and blue star-spangled costume in line with the fashion from the era. He also wore a tri-cornered hat and long cape. Much like his modern-day namesake, Rogers carried a shield.

JOSEPH AND SARAH ROGERS

Steve Rogers' parents, Joseph and Sarah Rogers, were of Irish-Catholic descent and made their home in the Brooklyn borough of New York City. Their son Steven was born on July 4, 1922. Joseph, a heavy drinker, died of a heart attack when Steve was very young, leaving Sarah to raise the boy by herself during the worst years of the Great Depression. Sarah worked in a garment factory and performed odd jobs to make ends meet, demonstrating the values of dedication and quiet courage to her son.

Living in poverty took its toll on Sarah. In 1935, when Steve was still a teenager, she was diagnosed with pneumonia and died.

DR. ABRAHAM ERSKINE

This brilliant scientist of German-Jewish descent was the mastermind behind the Super-Soldier formula. He created it to produce physically perfect human specimens who could fight Nazi forces during World War II. Steve Rogers, who had been rejected for military service due to his weak, sickly body, became Dr. Erskine's test subject and was the first success of Project: Rebirth. Sadly, an enemy spy assassinated the doctor mere moments after Rogers' transformation. Despite decades of research, no one has been able to precisely duplicate Erskine's formula.

IAN ZOLA

Mad scientist Arnim Zola created Ian in a test tube within the realm of Dimension Z. During his long exile in this other world, Steve Rogers rescued Ian and raised him from infancy to age 12. Ian learned Cap's fighting skills, including how to wield his famous shield, but was brainwashed by Arnim Zola. Ian was shot by Sharon Carter who mistook him for an enemy, but he regenerated to full health. Ian later became Nomad and partner to new Captain America, Sam Wilson.

GENERAL CHESTER PHILLIPS

As the US Army's liaison for scientific projects, General Phillips oversaw the creation of the military's top-secret Project: Rebirth. It was General Phillips who selected Steve Rogers to test the Super-Soldier formula. Phillips admired the young man's patriotism and fighting spirit. After Steve Rogers became Captain America, General Phillips acted as Cap's commanding officer and even borrowed a naval destroyer to search for Cap when he had gone missing.

ARNIE ROTH

During the 1930s, Arnie Roth was one of Steve Rogers' few friends, often sticking up for the smaller boy against Brooklyn bullies. When the United States entered World War II, Roth joined the Navy while Rogers became Captain America. Decades later, when Rogers emerged from suspended animation, an aged Arnie Roth became a friend once more, as well as a living link to the past that Rogers had lost.

BERNADETTE ROSENTHAL

Bernadette "Bernie" Rosenthal is a top lawyer and former girlfriend of Steve Rogers. Bernie met Steve while running her own business called "Rosenthal's Glass Menagerie" in New York City. The couple's relationship faltered due to Steve's commitment to his duties as Captain America, and Bernie subsequently left the city to study law at the University of Wisconsin-Madison. They remain friends.

BOBBY SHAW

When faced with the reality of combat during World War II, US Army private Bobby Shaw was weak and unsure, qualities that Captain America felt he could help Shaw overcome. Shaw served under Cap during operations in Tunisia, Italy, and elsewhere. He was often too terrified when pinned down by enemy fire to help his comrades. Ultimately, however, Cap's heroism rubbed off on Private Shaw, who suffered severe injuries from a Nazi grenade explosion. Shaw chose to remain behind and face certain death so that other soldiers could escape to safety.

SERGEANT MIKE DUFFY

To keep his activities secret from enemy spies, Steve Rogers posed as a regular soldier at Camp Lehigh in Virginia while secretly sneaking out to battle saboteurs as Captain America. Sergeant Mike Duffy—unaware of Rogers' double identity—took pleasure in tormenting Rogers and camp mascot Bucky for what he viewed as laziness and incompetence when they had in fact been out battling foes. Sergeant Duffy accompanied the Camp Lehigh soldiers to postings in England, Europe, and the Pacific, often getting himself into serious danger and only surviving thanks to Captain America.

DAVE COX

After losing his arm during his tour of duty, US military veteran Dave Cox became an antiwar protester and dedicated pacifist. He became friends with Captain America and had a hopeful romantic interest for Sharon Carter—though Carter did not share Cox's affections. When the Red Skull brainwashed Cox, Cap's friend became the costumed villain known as the Devil Slayer. Cap was able to defeat him, but Cox was left with serious injuries.

ALLIES

Many of Captain America's foes have opposed him since the days of World War II. Luckily for Cap, he has countless allies who will put their lives on the line to defend him against villains with long vendettas.

WINTER SOLDIER

James Buchanan "Bucky" Barnes was Captain America's sidekick during World War II. He spent years as a brainwashed Soviet assassin, codenamed the Winter Soldier. When Cap learned that Bucky had survived a deadly wartime explosion, he tried to find Bucky and reform him. Cap succeeded, and the rehabilitated Winter Soldier even adventured as Captain America when Steve Rogers was reportedly killed in action. After Rogers returned to the role of Cap, Bucky resumed his low-profile activities as the Winter Soldier.

FALCON

Sam Wilson grew up in New York City's Harlem, where he developed a love for birds and a streetwise fighting style. He met Captain America on a tropical island, teaming up with the hero to defeat the Red Skull. Afterward, Wilson assumed the heroic identity of the Falcon. Captain America and the Falcon made a great crime-fighting duo. Falcon helped Captain America track down the Winter Soldier, and later he nearly sacrificed his life to save New York City from a bomb launched by Cap's enemy Arnim Zola. Sam Wilson recently took on the identity of Captain America.

SHARON CARTER

Sharon Carter joined the espionage agency S.H.I.E.L.D. after being inspired by stories from her aunt and World War II agent Peggy Carter. For a time, Carter even worked as S.H.I.E.L.D.'s executive director. She teamed up with Cap on missions against the Red Skull and Hydra, and over time the two became romantically involved. Later, the villainous Dr. Faustus placed a hypnotic spell on Carter, causing her to shoot Captain America. But Cap did not perish. He reconciled with Sharon Carter as she took her revenge on Faustus and the Red Skull.

BATTLESTAR

Lemar Hoskins gained super-strength after he left the US Army. When his friend John Walker became the Super-Patriot, Hoskins and two other friends became his sidekicks. They were known as the Bold Urban Commandos. It wasn't long before the US government appointed Walker as the new Captain America. Hoskins briefly became the new Bucky. He later changed his name to Battlestar.

DEMOLITION MAN

Dennis Dunphy received strength-boosting treatments offered by the Power Broker, allowing him to compete in the superhuman Unlimited Class Wrestling Federation. Dunphy, however, wanted to be a Super Hero. He made his own costume and started calling himself Demolition Man, teaming up with Captain America to take down the Power Broker's illegal operation.

HAWKEYE

Clint Barton learned to shoot arrows in the circus. He later became a costumed adventurer and joined the Avengers. At first, he clashed with Cap, who was the leader of the Avengers. Hawkeye overcame his issues with Captain America, and saw him as a friend and mentor. They worked together for many years. Avengers Hawkeye, Cap, the Scarlet Witch, and Quicksilver became known as "Cap's Kooky Quartet."

JOHN JAMESON

Colonel John Jameson—the son of *Daily Bugle* publisher J. Jonah Jameson—is a veteran NASA astronaut who encountered a mysterious red gemstone on the surface of the moon. Jameson discovered that the stone had the power to transform him into the half-human Man-Wolf. Captain America signed Jameson up as a member of the Avengers support crew and often called on him to operate the team's Quinjets.

DIAMONDBACK

Rachel Leighton was smitten by Cap and often alerted him to danger. As Diamondback, she acted as a double agent for the Avengers and the villainous Secret Serpent Society, until she was put on trial for giving secrets to Captain America. Later, Diamondback was forced to steal blood from Cap, which would give the villains the power of his Super-Soldier serum. Through this they discovered that the formula was killing him, and Leighton risked her life to save Cap.

RICK JONES

As an honorary Avenger, Jones was present at Avengers Mansion when Captain America joined the team and quickly became one of Cap's closest friends. For a time, Rick Jones even became Captain America's new Bucky. When Captain America was believed to have been killed by an assassin, Rick Jones served as one of the pallbearers at Cap's funeral.

NOMAD (JACK MONROE)

When William Burnside became the new Captain America during the 1950s, Jack Monroe signed up as Burnside's sidekick Bucky. The duo spent decades in suspended animation, but after Burnside's death Jack Monroe decided to become a solo adventurer. Taking up the identity of Nomad—a role originally created by Steve Rogers—Monroe developed a talent for throwing stun-discs and helped Captain America fight Baron Zemo, the Red Skull, and Madcap.

PEGGY CARTER

During World War II, Peggy Carter served alongside French Resistance forces to sabotage the Nazi occupation and relay top-secret intelligence to Allied Command. Carter found herself working with the new Super-Soldier, Captain America, and the two fell in love. After the war, Peggy Carter worked with S.H.I.E.L.D. and in her old age she was reunited with Captain America following his return from suspended animation.

CAP'S TEAM-UPS

On his own, Captain America is a formidable force against the enemies of freedom. However, when he teams up with other heroes, Cap can achieve even greater deeds. From the wartime Invaders to the mighty Avengers, Cap has worked with some talented teammates.

THE AVENGERS

Formed to fight "the foes no single Super Hero can withstand," the original Avengers consisted of Iron Man, Thor, Ant-Man, the Wasp, and the Hulk—but it wasn't long before Captain America joined their ranks. The Avengers discovered Cap frozen in a block of Arctic ice, and they became a welcoming family for Steve Rogers after he awoke into a modern, unfamiliar world. Rogers jumped right back into the hero business, and with his military command experience, he quickly emerged as the Avengers' leader. Cap recruited Super Heroes Hawkeye, Quicksilver, and the Scarlet Witch, and presided over many other lineup changes in the years that followed. Captain America led the Avengers through such monumental events as the Kree–Skrull War, the emergence of Ultron, the time-traveling depredations of Kang the Conqueror, and the villainous team-up of the Masters of Evil.

Avengers Ant-Man and Thor are puzzled by the discovery of Steve Rogers' body.

Captain America might not have been the most physically powerful member of the Avengers team, but his steady leadership and clear honesty steered the Avengers through countless perils. In later years, Cap served with various incarnations of the Avengers, but he stepped away from the team when it dissolved following the Scarlet Witch's breakdown. After the events of the Superhuman Civil War—in which Super Heroes were divided over whether they should act under official government regulation—Captain America returned to lead various offshoot Avengers teams, including the classified Secret Avengers.

S.H.I.E.L.D.

The Strategic Homeland Intervention, Enforcement, and Logistics Division, or S.H.I.E.L.D., is a global intelligence-gathering and paramilitary organization. For years, Captain America's World War II comrade, Nick Fury, served as the agency's executive director, working closely with Cap and the Avengers on missions vital to global security. S.H.I.E.L.D. has virtually unlimited resources at its disposal, including gigantic Helicarriers and realistic androids called Life Model Decoys.

During Captain America's long affiliation with S.H.I.E.L.D. he has served as a liaison between the agency and the Super Hero community. Sharon Carter, a S.H.I.E.L.D. operative, worked closely with Cap on several missions and the two struck up a romance. For a time, S.H.I.E.L.D. fell under the control of the villain Norman Osborn. After Osborn's downfall, the US government appointed Captain America—in his non-costumed identity of Steve Rogers—as the agency's new overseer. In this role, Rogers rebuilt the organization with trusted operatives, installing Daisy Johnson—formerly the Avenger known as Quake—as the new executive director.

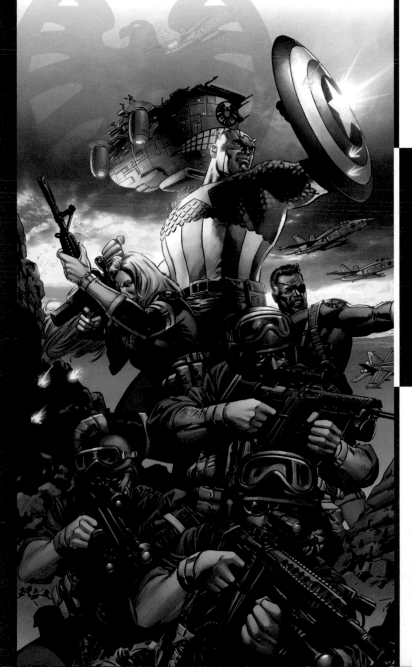

HOWLING COMMANDOS

Long before his time at S.H.I.E.L.D., a young Nick Fury joined the US Army after the attack on Pearl Harbor. He received command of the First Attack Squad—the so-called "Howling Commandos." The soldiers who made up this team of oddballs included Gabe Jones and "Dum Dum" Dugan. Captain America fought alongside the Howling Commandos during several engagements in the European Theater of Operations. Cap and Fury developed a deep, mutual respect.

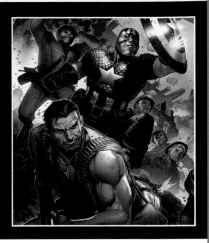

INVADERS

Faced with the threat of global aggression by the Axis powers, a team of super-powered heroes banded together during World War II and called themselves the Invaders. The team's original members included Captain America, Bucky, the Human Torch, Toro, and Namor the Sub-Mariner. The Invaders operated out of a mansion in England belonging to Lord Falsworth—also known as the hero Union Jack. The Invaders disbanded at the end of the war.

ALL-WINNERS SQUAD

After the end of World War II, a team called the All-Winners Squad carried on the work originally done by the Invaders. Its membership remained similar to the Invaders, but with one big change—the Captain America and Bucky in the All-Winners Squad were not Steve Rogers and Bucky Barnes, but rather their replacements: William Nasland and Fred Davis. Additional members of the All-Winners Squad included the Human Torch, Namor, Toro, Miss America, and the Whizzer.

ILLUMINATI

The Illuminati is a secret organization composed of some of the most intelligent and powerful figures on Earth who debate how to deal with serious global threats. Its original members were Super Heroes Iron Man, Professor X, Black Bolt, Doctor Strange, Reed Richards, and Namor. Captain America joined later, but was opposed to the Illuminati's idea of building an all-powerful weapon to protect Earth. Cap felt their actions were wrong and called for their arrest.

CAP'S SUPPORT NETWORK

Costumed heroes, international spies, and mercenaries are just some of the people who make up Captain America's vast support network. These are the characters that Cap relies on to feed him information, bail him out of trouble, and join forces with him against any major global threat.

CAPTAIN BRITAIN

Brian Braddock, a member of the British aristocracy, received the mantle of Captain Britain from the legendary wizard Merlyn. Using the power of the Amulet of Right—which he wore round his neck for a time—Captain Britain served as the champion of his homeland for many years, both on his own and in partnership with Captain America. He is currently a member of the secret group of intellectuals, the Illuminati.

BLACK WIDOW

Natasha Romanova was given the code name Black Widow by her Soviet bosses after receiving top-secret training in espionage. Sent to the United States to spy on Tony Stark's operations, she soon turned against her Russian controllers and teamed up with the Super Hero Hawkeye. Cap saw Black Widow's heroism, and supported her when she applied to join the Super Hero team the Avengers. She has also worked with the counter-terrorism agency, S.H.I.E.L.D.

IRON MAN

Tony Stark is the CEO of Stark Industries and one of the world's wealthiest and most famous people. Stark is also the legendary hero Iron Man. He helped found the Super Hero team the Avengers. Iron Man and Captain America are close friends, but their relationship has often been strained—especially during the "Civil War" over the Superhuman Registration Act, in which Iron Man and Cap joined opposing sides.

HUMAN TORCH (JIM HAMMOND)

When Professor Phineas T. Horton invented an android in the 1930s, he discovered that his creation's artificial skin ignited when exposed to oxygen. In time, Horton's "Human Torch" learned to control his flame powers, and assumed the identity of Jim Hammond. The Human Torch worked with Cap as a member of the Super Hero groups the Invaders, the All-Winners Squad, and then the Secret Avengers.

DOMINIC FORTUNE

A trained escapist and barnstorming pilot, the man known as Dominic Fortune was a hired mercenary during the 1930s. Prior to World War II, Fortune used his skills in combat and espionage to put down threats posed by Nazi villains such as Baron Zemo. Fortune was rejected as a test subject for the Super-Soldier program, but befriended chosen candidate Steve Rogers. He aided Rogers on his missions as Captain America.

MARIA HILL

Maria Hill was a long-serving agent of the security organization S.H.I.E.L.D. when she became its executive director. Despite a previously strained relationship—namely over Cap's refusal to comply with the US government's Superhuman Registration Act—Cap admired Hill's devotion to duty. When he received the opportunity to lead S.H.I.E.L.D., Cap named Hill as deputy. She later retook the top command post.

NAMOR

As the ruler of the undersea kingdom of Atlantis, Namor—aka the Sub-Mariner—is hostile toward surface-dwellers. In the early 1940s, he launched several attacks on New York City until he was stopped by the Human Torch (Jim Hammond). With the outbreak of World War II, Namor saw the threat posed by the Axis powers and joined the wartime Super Hero team the Invaders, along with Hammond and Captain America.

NICK FURY

During World War II, Nick Fury led a group of soldiers called the Howling Commandos, and was joined by Captain America during which time he developed a deep respect for Cap's fighting skills. After the war, Fury rose through the ranks of anti-terrorism agency S.H.I.E.L.D. and eventually reached the post of executive director. Fury and S.H.I.E.L.D. assisted Cap in his efforts to dismantle the terrorist group Hydra.

PALADIN

Paladin is a for-hire private investigator and soldier who packs a stun gun that can scramble a target's nervous system. Though not a villain, Paladin rarely does a good deed unless he is paid handsomely. His reputation as a skilled mercenary has made him a key member of Silver Sable's Wild Pack—a group set up to apprehend Nazi war criminals. Paladin joined Cap to defeat the criminal syndicate the Serpent Society.

SPIDER-MAN

Genius high-schooler Peter Parker received his super-powers after a bite from a spider that was radioactive. Realizing that his power came with great responsibility, Parker became the costumed hero known as Spider-Man. He has served alongside Cap during their mutual stints with the Avengers and Cap has helped Spider-Man resolve major incidents like Manhattan's transformation into "Spider Island."

THOR

Thor is the Norse God of Thunder who comes from the kingdom of Asgard. His father is Asgard's ruler, Odin, and his half-brother is the mischievous Loki. Thor wields an enchanted hammer named Mjolnir. Thought to be too proud, he was sent to Earth by his father, and took on the form of physician Donald Blake. Whenever danger loomed, he would transform into the God of Thunder. As one of the founding members of the Super Hero team the Avengers, Thor welcomed Cap like a brother.

UNION JACK

English aristocrat James Montgomery Falsworth first became Union Jack during World War I, executing missions for the British government. He continued his work during World War II, joining Cap and his costumed champions, the Invaders. Union Jack's career ended when his evil brother, a vampire named Baron Blood, crushed his legs with a boulder. Later, Cap put an end to the vampire's ways by decapitating him.

SPITFIRE

The daughter of Union Jack, young Jackie Falsworth was only a teenager when the vampire Baron Blood threatened Britain during World War II. Bitten by the Baron, Falsworth survived thanks to a rescue by Cap and an artificial blood transfusion from the Human Torch. She gained incredible speed, and became the costumed Super Hero, Spitfire. She joined the wartime Super Hero group the Invaders, led by Cap.

TORO

Thomas Raymond's parents worked as lab assistants for Professor Phineas T. Horton, the creator of the Human Torch. Their exposure to the android's artificial skin cells resulted in the boy's ability to cover his body in flame. As Toro, he was affiliated with a group that opposed Nazism, called the Young Allies. Soon after, he fought against the Axis powers in the Invaders, a team headed up by Captain America.

EVIL ORGANIZATIONS

Cap can always count on the Avengers to cover his back—but Super Heroes aren't the only ones who rely on the power of strength in numbers. Sinister groups like Hydra and A.I.M. also have a long list of members.

HYDRA

Hydra is one of the largest and most widespread criminal organizations on the planet. It is devoted to the overthrow of the world's governments and the establishment of a global dictatorship. The roots of Hydra's modern incarnation date back to World War II, when former Nazi officer Baron von Strucker seized control and grew it into an international powerhouse with a vast network of double agents and undercover spies. The organization proved to be masterful at mind control, and its brainwashed operatives—wearing their distinctive green uniforms—would relentlessly attack their enemies while shouting the infamous battle cry, "Hail Hydra!"

As a counterpoint to Hydra, the intelligence agency S.H.I.E.L.D. came into existence, with its director—former World War II veteran Nick Fury—becoming von Strucker's archenemy. Captain America has also opposed Hydra countless times, often assisting S.H.I.E.L.D. or the Avengers on missions to battle von Strucker, or to shut down a Hydra superweapon, such as the Death Spore bomb—designed to release a deadly biological agent.

A.I.M.

Advanced Idea Mechanics, or A.I.M., is a terrorist think tank composed of the most brilliant criminal scientists on Earth. A.I.M. began during World War II as a way for Baron von Strucker to obtain futuristic weapons for Hydra. Over the decades, A.I.M. scientists succeeded in making breakthroughs in the fields of genetic engineering, robotics, and theoretical physics. Among its creations was the super-power-mimicking android known as the Super-Adaptoid. A.I.M. also mutated one of its technicians into the ultra-genius M.O.D.O.K. (Mental Organism Designed Only for Killing). In more recent years, A.I.M. has moved to become a legitimate world power by taking control of the island nation of Barbuda, and earning a seat on the World Security Council.

Cap's shield offers little protection as A.I.M.'s Super-Adaptoid attacks him.

A.I.M. agents wear outfits resembling those worn by beekeepers, giving rise to the nickname "Beekeeper."

SERPENT SOCIETY

A business enterprise for costumed criminals dressed as snakes, the Serpent Society offers its members great benefits including profit sharing and access to advanced technology. The Society's members have included criminals such as Viper, Cottonmouth, Anaconda, Cobra, Princess Python, Sidewinder, Fer-de-Lance, Copperhead, and Diamondback. Captain America has fought various incarnations of the Serpent Society, opposing their hunt for the legendary Serpent Crown —a powerful and mystical ancient artifact—and preventing the transformation of the citizens of Washington, DC, into snake-people.

SONS OF THE SERPENT

A subversive organization dedicated to splitting the US along racial lines, the Sons of the Serpent was led by the Supreme Serpent—a military general named Chen who was visiting the US to speak before the United Nations. The organization carried out hate crimes against immigrants and racial minorities, culminating in Captain America's kidnap and the demand that Cap's Super Hero team of Avengers publicly agree with the group's racist beliefs. The Avengers rescued Cap and apprehended the criminals.

SUPER-AXIS

The Super-Axis was a World War II team of costumed Super Villains. Its members were loyal to the Axis powers of Nazi Germany and Imperial Japan. The group came into being to oppose Captain America and the World War II team of Super Heroes, the Invaders. Its members included Master Man, U-Man, Baron Blood, and Warrior Woman, under the organization of Japanese spy and hypnotist, Lady Lotus. Using her hypnotic powers, Lady Lotus controlled the Super-Axis to try to weaken the US during the war. Cap and his Invaders put an end to Lotus's plans.

MAGGIA

The Maggia is a loose confederation of crime families with roots in New York City. Cap has had a frustrating time fighting the Maggia, because the organization is careful to hide its activities, such as illegal gambling, to avoid prosecution.

SILVERMANE FAMILY

Wishing to prolong his life, "Silvermane" transferred his head onto a cyborg body. He was briefly the leader of terror group Hydra's operations on the US East Coast.

HAMMERHEAD FAMILY

"Hammerhead" had his skull smashed in a brawl and it was rebuilt using a steel alloy. He hopes to control crime in New York City, and is an enemy of Cap and Spider-Man.

NEFARIA FAMILY

Luchino Nefaria came from a long line of Italian nobility. His greed led him into crime. Cap fought Nefaria when the count trapped the Avengers inside his castle.

CAP'S ENEMIES

Over the years, Captain America has attracted a legion of foes, each one dedicated to bringing about his downfall.

AMERIDROID

Former Nazi scientist Lyle Dekker created a lifelike android twice the size of a human being and called it "Ameridroid." Dekker captured Cap and drained his power, diverting it into the 12-foot android. Dekker then transferred his mind into its body. Ameridroid and Cap fought several times, but the android sacrificed itself in an attempt to kill the Red Skull, who had betrayed it.

ANTI-CAP

The man known as the Anti-Cap was selected for a special program by the Office of Naval Intelligence. Believing it could replicate the Super-Solider process, the group placed an implant on Anti-Cap's spine that injected him with the super-steroid AVX. Ordered to carry out covert military missions, Anti-Cap fought the real Cap. It's thought he was killed by a train.

ARNIM ZOLA

Biochemist Arnim Zola served the Nazi regime during World War II, working alongside Super Villain the Red Skull to develop genetic monstrosities in the fight against freedom. Zola built a robotic construct to serve as his body, featuring a holographic face on its chest and a top-mounted "ESP box" used for mind control. Later, Cap found Zola hiding in a strange realm, Dimension Z, and managed to thwart Zola's invasion of Earth.

BATROC

Georges Batroc, a veteran of the French Foreign Legion, is an expert in the French kickboxing art of la savate. He operates as costumed mercenary Batroc the Leaper, performing missions for the highest bidder, but refusing to carry out crimes that violate his sense of honor. Batroc and Cap are enemies but also occasional allies, seen when Batroc, having trapped Cap, switched sides to help him fight evil group Hydra.

ALEKSANDER LUKIN

Aleksander Lukin was a former Soviet general who oversaw the deployment of Cap's former partner Bucky as the brainwashed assassin the Winter Soldier. Lukin used the Winter Soldier to kill the Nazi villain the Red Skull and steal the Cosmic Cube—a reality-bending object. Lukin's plan backfired when Cap, who was pursuing the Winter Soldier, recognized Bucky and used the Cosmic Cube to restore his friend's memories.

BARON HEINRICH ZEMO

Heinrich Zemo was a top Nazi scientist during World War II whose death ray cannons and other inventions were destroyed by Captain America and Nick Fury's group of soldiers, the Howling Commandos. Zemo invented Adhesive X—an unbreakable glue—and a fight with Cap caused the chemical to fix Zemo's hood to his face. He formed Super Villain team the Masters of Evil to oppose Cap's Avengers, but died in an avalanche.

BARON BLOOD

Angry when his older brother Montgomery inherited the family estate, Lord John Falsworth sought Dracula to gain the supernatural powers of a vampire. He acquired the codename Baron Blood while working for Germany during World War I, fighting his brother, the hero Union Jack. During World War II, Blood joined the Super-Axis team and fought Cap and the Invaders. In later years, Sam Wilson battled Blood as Cap, and killed him.

BARON STRUCKER

Baron Wolfgang von Strucker was a high-ranking Nazi officer during World War II, often fighting Captain America and his team of Super Heroes, the Invaders, as well as top soldier Nick Fury and his Howling Commandos. Following the war, Strucker took control of Hydra and set about transforming the organization into a worldwide criminal syndicate, with himself as the Supreme Hydra. Both Cap and Fury continued to oppose him.

BARON HELMUT ZEMO

The son of Baron Heinrich Zemo, Helmut always blamed Captain America for the death of his father. During a fight with Cap, Zemo fell into a vat of boiling glue, Adhesive X. His face was badly scarred and he covered it with a purple hood. In revenge, he kidnapped Cap's friends Arnie Roth and Dave Cox in order to lure Cap into a trap. Defeated by Cap, Zemo formed a new Masters of Evil and invaded Avengers Mansion.

MASTER MAN

During World War II in Germany, physically weak Wilhelm Lohmer volunteered for the Nazi version of the Super-Soldier program. The treatment made him even stronger than Cap, and Lohmer received the costumed identity of Master Man—the first specimen of what his commanders hoped would become a new master race. Master Man joined the Super-Axis and battled Cap and his group of wartime heroes, the Invaders.

FLAG-SMASHER

Karl Morgenthau was the son of a wealthy Swiss diplomat. Disgusted with the idea of nationalism and how it put certain groups of people above others, Karl created the costumed identity of Flag-Smasher. His aim was to topple the world's governments through terrorism. Cap opposed Flag-Smasher and the paramilitary network he led—ULTIMATUM, or the Underground Liberated Totally Integrated Mobile Army To Unite Mankind.

CROSSBONES

Brock Rumlow, better known as Crossbones, is the Red Skull's right-hand man. He is an expert combatant and sniper who usually carries throwing knives and a collapsible crossbow. It was Crossbones, working with a brainwashed Sharon Carter, who shot Captain America (Steve Rogers), apparently killing him. Later, Crossbones joined Hydra, fighting Sam Wilson in his role as the new Captain America.

DR. FAUSTUS

A brilliant psychologist and hypnotist, Austrian-born Dr. Faustus has opposed Cap and his allies both on his own and as a loyal servant of Hitler's protégé, the Red Skull. Among Faustus' crimes is his brainwashing of anti-terrorism agency S.H.I.E.L.D. member Sharon Carter, causing her to shoot Cap in a near-fatal incident. Eventually, Faustus grew weary of the Red Skull, and he informed S.H.I.E.L.D. about the villain's activities.

M.O.D.O.K.

George Tarleton, a technician working for global scientific terror group A.I.M. (Advanced Idea Mechanics), was subjected to mutagenics that resulted in his transformation into the super-intelligent M.O.D.O.C. (Mental Organism Designed Only for Computing). It wasn't long before Tarleton realized the extent of his power, seizing control of the organization and renaming himself M.O.D.O.K. (Mental Organism Designed Only for Killing).

SUPERIA

Inspired by the desire for a purely matriarchal future, scientist Deidre Wentworth called herself Superia and recruited an army of female Super Villains, the Femizons. They made their home on a shielded island, where Superia planned to launch "sterility seed" missiles that would leave her Femizons as the only women capable of repopulating the Earth. Captain America managed to put a stop to Superia's plan.

VIPER

Super Villain Madame Hydra killed the original founder of mercenary group the Serpent Squad and became its leader, Viper. Then she used her talents as a criminal strategist to rise to the top of the expanding nefarious business enterprise the Serpent Society. Viper later clashed with Captain America after infecting the water supply of Washington, DC, with a chemical that caused humans to mutate into snake creatures.

RED SKULL

The Red Skull was a symbol of Nazi propaganda during World War II, ideologically opposed to Cap, whom he fought many times. When the bunker in which he was fighting Cap collapsed, it released gases that put Red Skull into suspended animation. In the modern era, he re-emerged to discover that Cap had experienced a similar fate. Death has not stopped the Red Skull, who transplanted his mind into various bodies, even Cap's!

SIN

The daughter of Red Skull, Sinthea Shmidt received an artificial age boost in childhood that gifted her with telepathy and telekinesis. She took control of the Sisters of Sin—composed of other age-accelerated girls—as their Mother Superior. Following her defeat by Cap, Sinthea received mental reprogramming from anti-terror agency S.H.I.E.L.D., until she was freed by fellow villain Crossbones. She later called herself Sin.

SCOURGE OF THE UNDERWORLD

The Scourge of the Underworld is no single person, but an identity held by a succession of vigilantes, each dedicated to killing costumed criminals. Carrying a machine gun that fires explosive-tipped bullets and shouting a victory cry of "Justice is served," the Scourge of the Underworld is feared in Super Villain circles. Cap apprehended the first Scourge, only for him to be killed before he could reveal any secrets.

CAPTAIN AMERICA'S LOVES

Cap met and fell in love with Peggy Carter while she was fighting for the French Resistance during World War II.

While duty often comes first for Cap, that doesn't mean he has no time for love. He has dated several women over the years—and has been engaged more than once—although he is not yet ready to tie the knot.

BETSY ROSS

Betsy Ross was an agent for the FBI who became Steve Rogers' girlfriend during World War II. When the second Bucky (Fred Davis) was shot, Cap (then Jeffrey Mace) needed another costumed partner to assist him on his missions, and Betsy filled the role as Golden Girl. Betsy and Jeff married after they both retired from fighting crime.

PEGGY CARTER

Cap's greatest love in World War II was Peggy Carter, a young woman from Virginia who had gone to Europe before the US was involved in the war, to fight alongside the French Resistance. An exploding shell gave her amnesia, and it was decades before she was reunited with Cap—who had thought he would never see her again.

SHARON CARTER

Peggy Carter's stories of World War II heroism inspired her niece Sharon to join the anti-terrorism agency S.H.I.E.L.D. While working as Agent 13—a codename her aunt Peggy had worked under while aiding the French Resistance—she met and fell in love with Captain America (Steve Rogers). He proposed to her, but she was too committed to her job. Years later, Sharon proposed to Steve instead and she is still waiting for his response.

BERNIE ROSENTHAL

Steve Rogers met Bernie when she moved into his apartment building. Steve kept his identity as Cap secret from her, but she eventually figured it out. The two started dating and Bernie asked Cap to marry her, and he accepted. Cap, however, became so busy with fighting crime that Bernie called off their engagement. They remain friends.

RACHEL LEIGHTON

When Cap first met Rachel she was working with the criminal enterprise the Serpent Society and going by the name of Diamondback. She left her villainous ways and started helping out Cap, and their relationship became romantic for a time. After they broke up, Rachel worked with Steve Rogers as an agent of S.H.I.E.L.D. when the spy agency was under his command.

TIMELINE

- Steve Rogers is born on Manhattan's Lower East Side in 1922.

- A young Steve is protected from local bullies by his friend, Arnie Roth.

- Steve is orphaned following the death of his mother from pneumonia. His father had died several years earlier.

- Nick Fury helps scientist Abraham Erskine escape from Germany to the US. Erskine brings his secret Super-Soldier serum formula with him.

- When World War II starts, Steve repeatedly tries to join the army, but is rejected on health grounds. He signs up for Operation Rebirth.

- Operation Rebirth sees Steve transformed into the first Super-Soldier, only for a Nazi agent to kill Dr. Erskine, halting the project.

- Captain America tracks down Nazi spy Agent X, discovering that she is Cynthia Glass, Steve's first real girlfriend.

- On a mission to the African state of Wakanda, Captain America meets the Black Panther and is given a gift of the powerful metal Vibranium, which is later used to make his circular shield.

- Steve Rogers meets Bucky Barnes at US Army Camp Lehigh, and the teenager quickly becomes Cap's trusted sidekick.

- Captain America rescues the US President from an angry Prince Namor (the Sub-Mariner).

- Cap encounters Logan (later known as Wolverine) and the pair rescue a young Natasha Romanova (later the Black Widow) from Baron Strucker and the criminal organization known as the Hand.

- Namor, recognizing their common foe, joins up with Cap and the Human Torch to fight the Nazis and Master Man, who is Germany's answer to Captain America. They save British Prime Minister Winston Churchill, who names them "the Invaders."

- Cap fights alongside Nick Fury and the Howling Commandos.

- The Red Skull captures Cap and his allies. Bucky forms a new team—the Liberty Legion—to rescue them.

- Cap travels to England, where he fights Baron Blood and meets Spitfire and Union Jack, who later join the Invaders.

- Nazi scientist Baron Zemo is horrifically disfigured while fighting Cap. His mask becomes stuck to his face with Adhesive X—a substance of his own invention.

- While helping the French Resistance, Cap meets Peggy Carter (codename "Mademoiselle") for the first time. The two embark on a passionate love affair but are separated by the war.

- Steve briefly dates Adriana "Ana" Soria, the first female marine. Decades later she would become the villain known as the Queen.

- In the later stages of World War II, a showdown between the Red Skull and Cap leaves the villain seemingly dead, buried under rubble.

- Captain America helps the push in Europe, fighting at Omaha Beach and in the Battle of the Bulge, before pressing on to Berlin.

- When Baron Zemo launches a new drone plane, Captain America and Bucky manage to divert it, but its bomb explodes, sending them crashing into the ocean.

- Bucky's body is found by the Soviets.

- Cap becomes frozen in ice. Thanks to the Super-Soldier serum, the aging process is slowed and Cap is kept alive.

- In the final days of World War II, with Cap and Bucky believed dead, President Truman appoints William Nasland (aka Spirit of '76) to be the new Captain America.

- A year into his role as Cap, Nasland is killed and replaced as Captain America by Jeff Mace (the Patriot).

- Mace retires in 1950 and William Burnside—masquerading as Steve Rogers—becomes Captain America, while Bucky's role is taken by Jack Monroe.

- The new Captain America fights the Red Skull for the first time.

- Burnside and Monroe are placed in suspended animation when they become insane due to the fact that they lacked access to the necessary Vita-Rays when gaining their powers.

- Decades later, Namor the Sub-Mariner comes across an Inuit tribe worshipping a block of ice containing a human form. He hurls the block into the ocean, the ice melts, and the frozen Steve Rogers is rescued by the Avengers.

- Steve meets the Avengers for the first time. He returns to New York with them and helps to save the team from the D'Bari alien Vuk.

- Captain America becomes the first new member of the Avengers.

- As the Avengers search for the missing Hulk, Cap encounters the Fantastic Four.

- Cap takes on a mentor role to the Hulk's young friend, Rick Jones. Rick later briefly becomes a new Bucky alongside Cap.

- Baron Zemo comes out of retirement and assembles the Masters of Evil to attack his old enemy.

- Cap and the Avengers fight the time-traveling villain Kang the Conqueror for the first time.

- Wonder Man double-crosses the Masters of Evil and joins the Avengers, only to seemingly die shortly afterward.

- The Avengers and Cap team up with the original X-Men to fight the alien known as Lucifer.

- Kang creates a robot to impersonate Spider-Man and try to join the Avengers. Cap meets the real Spider-Man when Spider-Man rescues the team from his robotic duplicate.

- Cap and the Avengers fight Count Nefaria, the Italian crime lord, for the first time.

- Baron Zemo accidentally kills himself during a fight with Captain America and the Avengers.

• When the original members leave the Avengers, Cap is joined by Hawkeye and ex-Super Villains Quicksilver and the Scarlet Witch. He begins training this new crack team.

• Cap encounters Dr. Doom when the villain kidnaps the Avengers in order to lure the Fantastic Four into a trap.

• Cap remembers the Red Skull's wartime boast of "Der Tag": A future date when Nazi sleeper robots would awaken should the Allies win the war. He heads to Germany to destroy them.

• Steve meets S.H.I.E.L.D. agent Sharon Carter (Agent 13) and helps her retrieve a weapon from Batroc the Leaper, who would go on to consider Cap his archenemy.

• The Red Skull fights Cap for the first time since World War II, having been brought out of suspended animation by scientists from THEM, the group created by Baron Strucker that would soon become A.I.M. Two.

• Back with Nick Fury (now head of S.H.I.E.L.D.), Cap works with the agency against Hydra and A.I.M., but declines to be a full-time agent.

• Steve Rogers proposes to Sharon Carter, who turns him down to pursue her role as a S.H.I.E.L.D. agent.

• Cap reveals his secret identity to the world, but soon regrets it—it has made him an easy target for his enemies.

• In Wakanda, Cap fights alongside Black Panther—the kingdom's ruler—and an undercover Sharon Carter, to disarm a solar weapon.

• When Cap decides to leave the Avengers, he recommends the Black Panther as his replacement.

• Rick Jones takes on the role of Cap's old sidekick, Bucky.

• The Space Phantom makes the world forget that Steve Rogers is Captain America, as part of his plot against the Avengers.

• The Red Skull gains control of a Cosmic Cube and uses it to switch bodies with Cap. As Cap, the Red Skull causes Rick to quit as Bucky.

• While fighting the Red Skull's followers on Exile Island, Cap meets Sam Wilson and inspires him to become the hero known as the Falcon.

• For a cosmic competition with Kang, the Grandmaster sends some of the Avengers back in time to World War II, where they face off against the Invaders—led by a younger Captain America.

• Steve Rogers goes undercover to investigate missing police officers and defeats the villain Grey Gargoyle. He remains a cop so Steve Rogers can make a difference to the world just like Captain America.

• Cap and the Avengers help save Earth from the Kree–Skrull War.

• Cap fights alongside Sharon Carter and S.H.I.E.L.D.'s Femme Force against the Kingpin and Hydra, later learning that the Red Skull was behind his recent confrontations.

• William Burnside, the Captain America of the 1950s, is revived by a government official seeking to bring back the "Commie-bashing" hero, and Steve is forced to face his insane successor.

• Cap takes on Viper and the Serpent Squad for the first time. When the Super-Soldier serum reacts with one of Viper's poisons, Cap temporarily gains super-strength.

• Steve is reunited with wartime flame Peggy Carter when he rescues her and Sharon Carter from neo-Nazi psychiatrist Dr. Faustus.

• Cap faces off against the Sub-Mariner in the Avengers/Defenders war, before the two teams collaborate to fight Loki and Dormammu, Lord of the Dark Dimension.

• Baron Zemo's son, Helmut, attacks Cap. The villain calls himself Phoenix, but he later assumes his father's title.

• The Secret Empire frames Captain America for murder. He eventually traces their leadership back to the White House.

• Cap is pulled out of time by a future Rick Jones as part of a multiple-era Avengers event. He is later returned to the moment he left, with no memory of his adventure.

• Cap journeys to the future with Sharon Carter and the Thing to assist the Guardians of the Galaxy in a fight against the alien Badoon race.

• Joining up with old friends from the Liberty Legion, Cap helps put a stop to the Whizzer's son, Nuklo.

• Disillusioned by his knowledge of who was running the Secret Empire, Steve Rogers quits his role as Captain America, but soon assumes a new identity—Nomad.

• Nomad teams up with the Sub-Mariner to prevent Viper and the Serpent Squad getting hold of the powerful Serpent Crown.

• A young man called Roscoe briefly becomes Captain America, only to be slain by the Red Skull. Steve Rogers reprises the role once more.

• The Red Skull reveals that he played a role in Sam Wilson becoming Cap's sidekick. But the Falcon overcomes the Red Skull's brainwashing and remains a hero.

• Steve is taken on a journey through American history, gaining insight into the meaning of his role as Captain America.

• Captain America teams up with Captain Britain to thwart a plan by the Red Skull to destroy London.

• Back in the US, Cap stops the Royalist Forces of America unleashing their "Madbomb" and driving the country's citizens insane.

• Cap and Sharon face Dr. Faustus's National Force, whose puppet leader is an insane William Burnside, the 1950s Captain America.

• Sharon Carter is seemingly killed after infiltrating National Force.

• Cap considers running for President, but decides against it.

• During a mission to England, Cap is reunited with Spitfire, meets the new Union Jack, and once more faces Baron Blood.

• Steve starts a relationship with his neighbor Bernadette "Bernie" Rosenthal and runs into his childhood friend Arnie Roth.

• Helmut Zemo adopts his father's name—Baron Zemo.

• Cap helps Jack Monroe (the 1950s Bucky) to overcome his madness and Monroe briefly becomes Cap's partner as a new Nomad.

• Captain America travels to a future Earth to fight alongside the cyborg Deathlok against the dictator Hellinger.

• Bernie, who now knows Cap's identity, proposes to Steve.

• Cap is one of numerous heroes and villains transported from Earth to Battleworld to fight each other at the behest of the Beyonder.

• While on Battleworld, Cap's shield is damaged. Thanks to Battleworld's strange physics he is able to fix it.

• Cap is enraged when he believes the Red Skull has killed his friends and allies, including Bernie. After they battle, the Skull almost dies of old age, but is kept alive by Nazi scientist Arnim Zola, who places the Skull's consciousness into a Steve Rogers clone.

• When the Vision seizes control of the world's computer systems, Cap and the Avengers are forced to confront their teammate.

• Nomad quits his partnership with Cap and leaves New York.

• Sidewinder forms the Serpent Society, a group of snake-themed bad guys that Cap fights on several occasions.

• Steve sets up Captain America's Hotline to allow regular Americans to report potential threats.

• Cap recruits Prince Namor into the Avengers.

• The Avengers help Daredevil stop the rampage of a failed Super-Soldier, Nuke, which was orchestrated by the Kingpin.

• Bernie ends her relationship with Steve and leaves New York.

• Cap fights the Super-Patriot (John Walker) and starts to question his role as Captain America.

• Baron Zemo and the Masters of Evil launch an audacious attack on Avengers Mansion. Zemo taunts Cap by destroying his wartime possessions, leading to a violent showdown.

• Cap and Nomad team up to stop the Florida drug-dealer, Slug.

• Demolition Man (also known as D-Man) and Cap discover that the Power Broker is helping the US government create new Super-Soldiers.

• Cap takes on G.I. Max, the government's latest Super-Soldier.

• The Commission for Superhuman Activities tries to coerce Steve Rogers into working for them as Captain America. Steve resigns, handing back his uniform and shield.

• The Commission appoints John Walker as the new Captain America.

• Steve assumes the identity of "The Captain" and forms a team with Nomad, Falcon, and D-Man.

• The Captain receives a new Vibranium shield from the Black Panther.

• The Captain leads a team of ex-Avengers against the powerful, insane geneticist the High Evolutionary.

• D-Man seemingly dies in battle while helping Steve take on the villainous ULTIMATUM group.

• The Captain fights when hordes of demons swarm through New York. A new team of Avengers forms when the battle is over.

• Cap reveals the Red Skull had been manipulating the Commission on Superhuman Activities. After a showdown with his replacement, Steve returns to his role as Captain America and John Walker takes the Captain's black uniform to become U.S. Agent.

• Steve teams up with reformed villain Diamondback and they become romantically involved.

- Captain America leads the Avengers into space to protect Earth during the Kree–Shi'ar war.

- Steve is changed into a werewolf while fighting Dredmund Druid and Nightshade.

- As a side effect of the "Infinity War" raging across the world, "Capwolf" has to fight an evil double of Captain America.

- Cap helps Spider-Man to defeat the insane alien symbiote Carnage.

- Ignoring the UN's command, Cap takes the Avengers to Genosha to rescue Quicksilver and Crystal's daughter, Luna, from Magneto's former associates.

- Cap learns that the Super-Soldier serum is endangering his life. He continues to fight, but takes on two assistants—Free Spirit and Jack Flag—as potential successors.

- Cap is sustained by Stark-built exoskeletal armor as his health deteriorates. He eventually appears to die in Avengers Mansion—only for his body to vanish.

- The Red Skull revives Captain America, who prevents Hate-Monger (a clone of Adolf Hitler) from creating a Nazi-dominated world. Cap discovers Sharon Carter is still alive.

- Machinesmith frames Captain America for leaking military secrets, forcing the President to strip Steve Rogers of his US citizenship until he is able to prove his innocence.

- Onslaught claims the lives of several heroes—including Captain America—who then reappear on an alternate Earth created by Franklin Richards, the son of Mr. Fantastic and the Invisible Woman.

- On this Counter-Earth, Steve Rogers is a happily married man with a child—until Nick Fury reveals that Steve's family are robots and Steve is really Captain America. Eventually Cap and his fellow heroes learn the truth and return to their own world.

- Almost everyone who has ever been an Avenger joins battle against Morgan le Fay, only to become transplanted to her medieval realm. Cap leads his teammates against the sorceress and breaks her spell. Following the battle, a new Avengers line-up is announced.

- Cap loses his shield in the Atlantic Ocean while fighting Hydra. He is given the museum replica of his original triangular shield, then later uses one made of energy, before finally getting his own shield back.

- A Skrull warrior impersonates Cap and incites Americans to riot.

- Cap objects when Tony Stark uses advanced telepathy to erase the knowledge of Iron Man's identity from the world.

- Cap trains the Redeemers: A group of reformed villains who are working for the government.

- When Kang conquers the Earth, the Avengers are forced to surrender. Cap and a handful of heroes return to Earth to help defeat Kang.

- Cap befriends the aging Isaiah Bradley: an African-American subject of Super-Soldier serum tests in World War II.

- Another attempt at a Super-Soldier—the Anti-Cap—battles Cap.

- When the Scarlet Witch goes insane and attacks her teammates, several Avengers end up dead and the team is disbanded.

TIMELINE

- Depressed by the demise of the Avengers, Cap reignites his relationship with Diamondback—only to discover this version is a robot.

- Cap encounters Ana Soria again for the first time since World War II. Now a Super Villain known as the Queen, she attacks Spider-Man, who defeats her with Cap's help.

- Cap learns that the Red Skull has been assassinated.

- The Winter Soldier, a deadly assassin whom Cap has been tracking, turns out to be Bucky Barnes. Cap uses the Cosmic Cube to free his old partner from his Soviet programming, but Bucky flees in horror as his memories return.

- When a mass breakout at the Raft prison brings several heroes together, Cap convinces them to form a new Avengers team.

- Cap is alarmed when he comes across the Young Avengers. He tries in vain to put a stop to them, but later becomes their mentor.

- In an alternate reality created by the Scarlet Witch, Steve Rogers didn't enter suspended animation and is now an old man. He returns to normal when the Scarlet Witch restores reality.

- Captain America and the Winter Soldier are reunited in London when the city is attacked by the Red Skull.

- As the federal government passes the Superhuman Registration Act, Cap finds himself leading those opposed to it in what quickly becomes the Superhuman Civil War.

- A wanted man, Cap forms the Secret Avengers to oppose Tony Stark's pro-registration forces in the civil war.

- In a final showdown with the government-backed heroes, Cap realizes he is endangering the public, so he surrenders and is arrested.

- Steve Rogers is assassinated as he goes to trial.

- Tony Stark receives a letter from Steve Rogers stating that, if he dies, Stark should help Bucky ensure the legacy of Captain America lives on.

- Bucky fights Iron Man but eventually agrees to be Captain America.

- The new Cap, Sharon, and Falcon learn that Steve is alive, but has been frozen in space and time.

- The new Cap, Sharon, and Falcon try to rescue Steve, who is "unstuck" in time, jumping between key moments of his life, as he makes his way back to the present and his own body—just in time to stop the Red Skull taking possession of it.

- Steve decides Bucky has earned the right to remain Captain America after they defeat the Super Villain, Hyde.

- The President pardons Cap for his role in the Superhuman Civil War.

- Steve briefly becomes Captain America again to protect Asgard from Norman Osborn's forces when they lay siege to the city.

- Having been made director of S.H.I.E.L.D. by the President, Steve assembles new Avengers teams, including a covert strike force (the Secret Avengers) that he leads himself.

- Steve joins the secret team of Illuminati and is given possession of the Time Gem, one of the cosmically powerful Infinity Gems.

- When Cul Borson, the Asgardian God of Fear (aka the Serpent), attacks Earth, Bucky apparently dies and Steve becomes Cap again.

- Captain America's shield is broken during the fighting with Cul Borson, but Tony Stark repairs it using Asgardian tech. Although scarred, it is now stronger than ever before.

- Cap is one of the few people who learns that Bucky survived the fight against the Serpent and that he became the Winter Soldier again.

- Steve is captured by the Jackal and mutated into a giant arachnid creature—the Spider-King—who is controlled by the Queen (Ana Soria), until he is changed back by Spidey and his allies.

- When Cap learns that the cosmic entity known as Phoenix Force is returning to Earth, the Avengers confront the X-Men in an attempt to gain custody of Hope Summers, who they believe will be the entity's host. This act starts a war between the X-Men and the Avengers.

- In the aftermath of the war, Cap assembles an Avengers Unity Division made up of mutants and Avengers, in order to show how humans and mutants can live and work together.

- Cap and the Avengers take on Venom when the symbiote possesses the Superior Spider-Man.

- Captain America travels to Dimension Z—a parallel reality created by Arnim Zola. Cap escapes Zola's base, taking the young child of Zola with him, whom he raises as his own son called Ian.

- After years trapped in Dimension Z, Cap returns home, leaving behind Sharon Carter, who came to rescue him, and the now teenage Ian.

- Cap and Iron Man put together a new Avengers team and soon face an attack from the Mad Titan, Thanos.

- Sharon Carter and Ian escape Dimension Z and are reunited with Cap.

- In a fight with the tentacled Iron Nail, the Super-Soldier serum is drained from Steve's body. Steve quickly starts to age.

- Forced to step back from the front line, Steve makes Sam Wilson (Falcon) his successor as Captain America.

- The new Captain America and other heroes become temporarily evil following a misfired spell by the Scarlet Witch. Steve Rogers dons a powersuit to lead a group of similarly reformed villains against the corrupted Avengers.

- Sam Wilson fights Baron Blood as Captain America.

- Steve learns that an alien incursion threatens Earth, but the Super Heroes are powerless to stop it.

- The world ends and is recreated by Dr. Doom as Battleworld; a place where an alternate version of Steve Rogers finds himself a gladiator in an arena, with no memory of any other life.

- Following the heroes' return from Battleworld, Captain America (Sam Wilson) becomes part of an all-new Avengers team, while the venerable Steve Rogers acts as an advisor to Super Heroes. Who knows what the future holds for Cap?

THE 19

In the 1940s, many countries became embroiled in World War II, and Captain America was created to become America's greatest and most inspiring hero.

In early 1940—with much of the world already at war—Joe Simon and Jack Kirby knew that the US needed a hero to embody the nation's values as it was drawn into the largest conflict the globe had ever seen. They came together to create Captain America for their new employer, Timely Comics (the company that would eventually become Marvel). The company had already had some success with the brand-new genre of Super Hero comics featuring the Human Torch and the Sub-Mariner. Joe and Jack wrapped their new wartime hero in patriotic red, white, and blue.

Readers quickly embraced the all-American hero and devoured his wartime exploits. Early issues of *Captain America Comics* sold nearly a million copies, and New York Mayor Fiorello La Guárdia was reputedly a fan. When American G.I.s went off to war, many of them took copies of *Captain America Comics* with them. Jack went off to serve in the US Army, and Joe enlisted in the US Coast Guard, but not before Timely's publisher, Martin Goodman, arranged for them to supply a year's worth of Captain America stories, so the hero could continue his adventures after they left.

OVERLEAF

Captain America Comics #16 (July 1942): After escaping jail and learning to become a skilled archer, the Red Skull made a comeback. Armed with poison-tipped arrows, America's most fiendish menace presented a very real threat to Cap and Bucky. Penciler: Don Rico

40s

AMERICA STRIKES BACK

When the US entered World War II, Captain America and Bucky became heroes for American soldiers to rally around. Leading from the front, they wiped out Hitler's spies, and took the fight to Japan after the surprise attack on Pearl Harbor at the end of 1941.

CAP AT WAR

Captain America was created as a World War II hero—but his role didn't end with the war. Over the next few years, Cap and Bucky had plenty of adventures and faced many challenges.

CAP LIVES ON

After the original Cap and Bucky were thought to have been killed by Baron Heinrich Zemo, William Nasland—formerly a hero known as the Spirit of '76—adopted Cap's uniform, though carrying a substitute shield. Fred Davis Jr.—a batboy for the New York Yankees—took over the role of the new Bucky, and joined the All-Winners Squad.

ALL-WINNERS

After the war ended, Cap and Bucky joined the Human Torch, Toro, Sub-Mariner, Whizzer, and Miss America on their first joint adventure. Working together for the first time as a team—the All-Winners Squad—they had to hunt down a master criminal called Isbisa, who sent them to stop a series of crooks while he tried to steal an atomic bomb.

CAP NUMBER 3

Not long after, William Nasland, still working as Captain America, was killed in action. Another hero, Jeffrey Mace (aka the Patriot) took over the costume and shield, and joined Fred Davis Jr. to become part of the All-Winners Squad.

A NEW PARTNER

Bucky (Fred Davis Jr.) was shot while trying to stop a robbery. Cap (Jeffrey Mace) trained Betsy Ross—who had worked with the FBI as a liaison to both Steve Rogers and William Nasland—to become Golden Girl, his brand-new partner in fighting crime. After they retired from being heroes, they got married.

CAPTAIN AMERICA
COMICS #3

No. 3 **CAPTAIN AMERICA** **MAY** **10¢**
COMICS

45 thrilling PAGES of CAPTAIN AMERICA PLUS OTHER FEATURES...

The RED SKULL planned a Horrible Death for BUCKY and BETTY -unless....

May 1941

COVER ARTIST
Alex Schomburg

WRITERS
Joe Simon, Jack Kirby, and Stan Lee

PENCILERS
Joe Simon, Jack Kirby, Mac Raboy ("Atlantis and the False King"), and Reed Crandall ("Satan and the Subway Disaster")

INKERS
Joe Simon, Jack Kirby, Al Avison, Al Gabriele, Bernie Klein, George Roussos, Reed Crandall, and Mac Raboy

LETTERER
Unknown

"This time the Red Skull will show no mercy!" THE RED SKULL

Main characters: Captain America; Bucky Barnes; the Red Skull **Supporting characters:** The Butterfly; Major Douglas; Sgt. Duffy; Midge **Main locations:** New York City; Ebbets Field; Camp Lehigh

BACKGROUND The first issue had been a bestseller, but by *Captain America* #3, Timely publisher Martin Goodman knew the company had a smash hit on its hands. Goodman soon had creators Joe Simon and Jack Kirby working in-house, the prolific Kirby penciling quality page after quality page. Kirby, born Jacob Kurtzberg on Manhattan's Lower East Side, had an impoverished upbringing and took up art as a means to escape a life of factory work and gang fights. He teamed up with Joe Simon when they were both working at Max Fleischer's animation studios. In these early days of comics, creators' names were never in the spotlight, and they were often assisted by other artists to help maximize output. Comic book historians have done a great job of giving credit where it's due, but in some cases—such as this issue's letterer—names remain unknown.

A few weeks before work began on *Captain America* #3, Timely had gained another new employee, teenager Stanley Lieber, who was the cousin of Martin Goodman's wife. Learning the ropes alongside Kirby and Simon, he was given his first writing gig for *Captain America*'s third issue—the text story "Captain America Foils the Traitor's Revenge," which joined three Cap strips and three more, unrelated strips. The inclusion of text stories let Timely take advantage of the cheaper postage rates given to magazines. Lieber used a pseudonym for his story—Stan Lee. By *Captain America* #10, Kirby and Simon had left the company after falling out with Goodman, and the 18-year-old Stan Lee found himself in a new role—editor of Timely Comics.

THE STORY

The Red Skull returns and only Captain America and Bucky can stop his devastating attack on New York. Meanwhile, the duo also deal with Cap and Bucky look-alikes, a master criminal, and a traitorous soldier.

1

2

3

4

The Red Skull rose to his feet **(1)**, having faked his death at the end of his first encounter with Cap. More determined than ever to strike at the heart of the United States, the villain stole plans for a huge drilling machine from Major Douglas, killing him with his new "death touch." Steve Rogers and Bucky Barnes arrived just afterward and found the Red Skull's mask there—a sign that their old enemy was responsible. Nazi thugs tried to ambush the heroes but were quickly dealt with. However, Cap and Bucky were unable to stop the Red Skull's attack a few days later. A gigantic drilling machine, piloted by the Skull himself, exploded out of the ground and went on to devastate the city, killing thousands. Cap and Bucky caught up with it as it launched an attack on a crowded football stadium. They couldn't stop it, but did manage to chase it away.

Meanwhile, gangsters Duffer and Midge set up a scam to impersonate Cap and Bucky for money. Unfortunately for them, Cap and Bucky learned of their plan and put an end to the con. The criminals' luck ran out for good when the Red Skull, unaware that they were imposters, captured the pair and hanged them. The real Cap and Bucky confronted the Red Skull shortly afterward. Bucky, having realized that the "death touch" was an electric shock given off by the Skull's gloves, had insulated his own gloves to protect himself. The Red Skull tried to flee, throwing a bomb at the heroes **(2)**, but Cap hurled it back at the Skull, blowing up the villain and his machine. Later, Cap and Bucky stopped a Nazi killer loose on a movie set near Camp Lehigh, which had Steve dressing up as a knight to track the killer down.

While on guard duty at a later date, Rogers witnessed Colonel Stevens arguing with a disgraced soldier called Lou Haines, and helped escort Haines from the camp after he threatened the colonel. Rogers was in his tent later, playing checkers with Bucky, when he heard a noise outside the colonel's tent. Going to check, they saw Haines and some hired thugs creeping in. Realizing Haines was a traitor and intended to kill the colonel, Cap hurled his shield at Haines—leaping on the traitor and finishing him off with a ferocious punch **(3)**. While Cap dealt with Haines, Bucky captured his accomplices, and they were already tied up by the time Cap left the tent. Cap and Bucky left a note with the captured villains, explaining that they were a present from Captain America.

Their next adventure saw Cap and Bucky foil a notorious criminal known as the Butterfly, who was stealing ancient Egyptian treasures from the museum. The thief turned out to be the museum's curator, Doctor Vitroli, helped by his brute of an assistant, Lenny **(4)**. While the villainous pair managed to capture Bucky and trap him in a sarcophagus, they proved no match for Captain America himself.

BUCKY BARNES

Young James Buchanan "Bucky" Barnes discovered Steve Rogers had a secret identity, and soon after joined him as Captain America's costumed sidekick, Bucky. He was thought to have been killed during World War II, but he returned decades later as the Winter Soldier. He even took on the role of Cap for a time.

Bucky Barnes was Cap's original sidekick during World War II. Over the years, the role of Bucky has also been taken by former New York Yankee bat boy Fred Davis, a young Jack Monroe, and the Hulk's friend Rick Jones.

ORIGINS

Bucky's father was a soldier at Camp Lehigh in Virginia. He had enlisted before the outbreak of World War II, but he died during training, leaving Bucky orphaned aged only 15. Bucky was able to stay on because the rest of the camp adopted him as an unofficial mascot. Soon after, Bucky accidentally walked in on Steve Rogers as he was changing into his Captain America costume. With the consent of the Army, teen Bucky joined Steve in his training and became Captain America's sidekick.

A young Bucky Barnes discovers Steve Rogers in his Captain America uniform.

During the war, Bucky fought with Cap alongside the Invaders, and led his own team of teenage soldiers called the Kid Commandos. He also joined the Liberty Legion (a homefront version of the Invaders) and another group of teenage heroes, the Young Allies. Toward the end of the war, Cap and Bucky tried to stop the villain Baron Heinrich Zemo from destroying an experimental drone plane that had been filled with explosives. Cap and Bucky reached the plane, but it exploded before they could defuse it, apparently killing both heroes.

Bucky was plunged into the icy waters of the North Atlantic. A Soviet submarine found his frozen body—missing its left arm—and brought him back to Moscow to be revived. Scientists discovered Bucky was now suffering from amnesia, although he still retained his military skills. Under the direction of the KGB, he was given a bionic arm and brainwashed into becoming a Soviet assassin known as the Winter Soldier.

Between missions as a Soviet agent, Bucky was kept cryogenically frozen so he aged little over the decades. In modern times, the revived Captain America was troubled to discover that the Winter Soldier was actually his old friend Bucky. Steve tracked him down and used a Cosmic Cube to restore his lost memories. Now Bucky works tirelessly to redeem himself for his past murderous actions.

> ## "It's the Captain and I against all enemies of liberty!" BUCKY BARNES

As the Soviet-controlled Winter Soldier, Bucky carried out many missions against the US, including exploding a bomb in Philadelphia as part of a scheme to seize the Cosmic Cube for the Soviets.

The Winter Soldier trained Soviet operative Natasha Romanova, aka the Black Widow. The pair undertook missions together and became lovers, though she was required to marry Soviet test pilot Alexi Shostakov.

DATA FILE

FIRST APPEARANCE: *Captain America Comics* #1 (March 1941)

REAL NAME: James Buchanan "Bucky" Barnes

AFFILIATIONS: Avengers, Invaders, Liberty Legion, Kid Commandos, Young Allies.

POWERS AND ABILITIES: Bucky is an expert soldier and combatant. As the Winter Soldier, he is also a skilled assassin and has a bionic arm that grants him superhuman strength.

Bucky's bionic arm is painted with the same star symbol as the one on Cap's shield.

Unlike Cap, Bucky often uses weapons on missions.

THE NEW CAPTAIN AMERICA

Upon the conclusion of the Civil War, the original Captain America was assassinated. After his death, Iron Man found a letter from Steve Rogers, which included two requests: That the legacy of Captain America should live on, and that Bucky should be taken care of. Iron Man honored Steve's wishes by asking Bucky to become the new Captain America. When he took over as Cap, Bucky didn't feel fit to wear Steve's costume, so he fashioned himself a new one with the help of Tony Stark. For a short while after Steve returned from death, both he and Bucky served as Cap. When the world believed Bucky had died after battling Sin, he returned to his Winter Soldier identity.

THE RED SKULL

Handpicked by Adolf Hitler to become the perfect Nazi, young Johann Shmidt was transformed from an orphaned runaway into the greatest living symbol of the Third Reich. His hatred of US patriotism and heroism put him into direct conflict with Captain America in World War II, and their struggle continues to this day.

ORIGINS

Johann Shmidt's mother died during childbirth and his father committed suicide soon after. He grew up in an orphanage in Germany, but escaped to a life of crime on the streets. Johann became a paid assassin in his youth and later joined the Nazi party as a Brownshirt. He plotted with his boyhood friend Dieter Lehmann to murder Hitler in 1934. Dressing as a bellboy at the hotel the Führer was staying in, Johann, together with Lehmann, entered the room to carry out their plan, but at the last moment, Johann betrayed Dieter and shot him instead in front of Hitler.

Impressed by Johann's cold-hearted brutality, Hitler took Johann under his wing and ordered the SS to train him to become the Reich's greatest soldier. Unsatisfied with the training Johann was receiving, Hitler decided to take over the youth's training personally. Hitler made Johann wear a red skull mask to set him apart from his other officers. He was named the Red Skull and became an operative answerable only to Hitler.

Johann often sent out imposters on missions for him, having them wear a copy of his mask. They clashed with Captain America several times before Johann and Cap actually met in person. They fought in the last days of the war culminating in a confrontation in Hitler's bunker in Berlin, during which Cap narrowly escaped a tunnel collapse that was thought to bury alive the Red Skull.

In fact, Johann was saved by support pillars criss-crossing the bunker. The collapse triggered the release of an experimental gas from canisters within the bunker which put Johann into suspended animation for decades. He remained preserved in that way until the international terrorism group Hydra revived him to continue his battle against Cap, whom the Avengers had also recently discovered preserved in ice.

Soon after his revival Johann sought an heir to continue his tyranny, and so fathered a daughter, Sinthea, aka Sin. She later became the new Red Skull.

Young Johann joined the Nazi party and was trained to be the Reich's greatest soldier.

An American industrialist named George Maxon betrayed his country for the Nazis, posing as the Red Skull. He was defeated by Captain America.

Soviet spy Albert Malik became the Communist Red Skull of the 1950s. He ordered the deaths of Richard and Mary Parker, whose son Peter later became Spider-Man.

"Only the Red Skull still remains…to fulfil the Nazi dream!" THE RED SKULL

A revived clone of the Red Skull set out to exterminate all mutants. When powerful mutant Magneto tried to kill him, the Red Skull transformed into Red Onslaught, a combination of Magneto, the exceptional telepath Professor X, and the Red Skull himself.

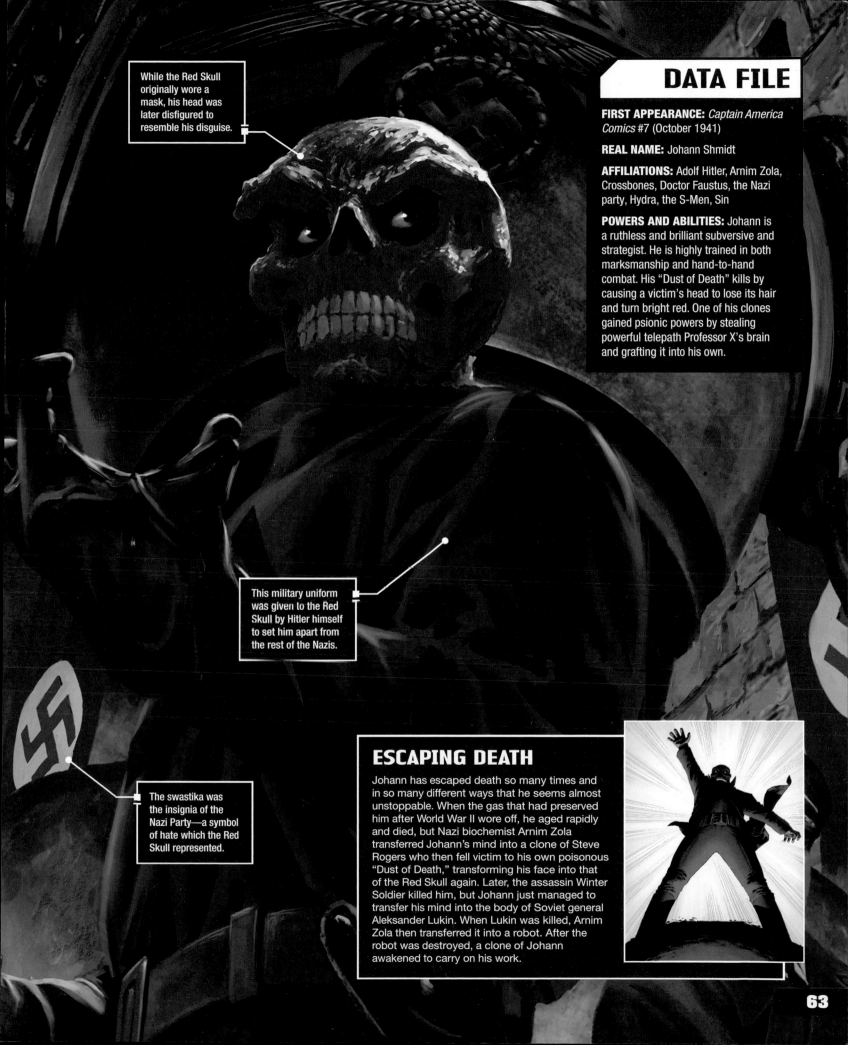

While the Red Skull originally wore a mask, his head was later disfigured to resemble his disguise.

DATA FILE

FIRST APPEARANCE: *Captain America Comics* #7 (October 1941)

REAL NAME: Johann Shmidt

AFFILIATIONS: Adolf Hitler, Arnim Zola, Crossbones, Doctor Faustus, the Nazi party, Hydra, the S-Men, Sin

POWERS AND ABILITIES: Johann is a ruthless and brilliant subversive and strategist. He is highly trained in both marksmanship and hand-to-hand combat. His "Dust of Death" kills by causing a victim's head to lose its hair and turn bright red. One of his clones gained psionic powers by stealing powerful telepath Professor X's brain and grafting it into his own.

This military uniform was given to the Red Skull by Hitler himself to set him apart from the rest of the Nazis.

The swastika was the insignia of the Nazi Party—a symbol of hate which the Red Skull represented.

ESCAPING DEATH

Johann has escaped death so many times and in so many different ways that he seems almost unstoppable. When the gas that had preserved him after World War II wore off, he aged rapidly and died, but Nazi biochemist Arnim Zola transferred Johann's mind into a clone of Steve Rogers who then fell victim to his own poisonous "Dust of Death," transforming his face into that of the Red Skull again. Later, the assassin Winter Soldier killed him, but Johann just managed to transfer his mind into the body of Soviet general Aleksander Lukin. When Lukin was killed, Arnim Zola then transferred it into a robot. After the robot was destroyed, a clone of Johann awakened to carry on his work.

American Peggy wears French clothing—including a beret—in order to blend in successfully.

DATA FILE

FIRST APPEARANCE: *Tales of Suspense* #77 (May 1966)

REAL NAME: Margaret "Peggy" Carter

AFFILIATIONS: Captain America, the French Resistance, S.H.I.E.L.D.

POWERS AND ABILITIES: Peggy is an excellent unarmed combatant. She is a skilled markswoman and can use the garotte. She is fluent in French.

Peggy is an able markswoman and is adept at using high-powered firearms, such as this submachine gun.

AN AGENT OF HER OWN

After World War II, Peggy suffered from amnesia. This would come and go, leaving her with long years of clarity and full memories. During those times, she often worked with Howard Stark—Iron Man's father. Peggy had worked with the S.H.I.E.L.D. engineer and inventor during World War II, but in the years that followed, Howard called upon her again to assist him on many dangerous missions—including dealing with alien technology!

Utility belt contains items needed in battle, and like the rest of the uniform, is dark colored for covert operations.

PEGGY CARTER

Unlike Cap, who had been preserved for decades, Peggy had continued to age. Despite her amnesia, she recognized him the moment she saw him.

Born to a wealthy family in Virginia, Peggy left home as a teenager to join the French Resistance, long before America joined the war. This brave and skillful resistance fighter, known as Agent 13, or simply "Mademoiselle," met and fell in love with Captain America. Promising to meet again, their paths did not cross for decades.

"This war was everybody's war. I was needed, and I answered the call."

PEGGY CARTER

While working for S.H.I.E.L.D., Peggy fought against the evil terrorist organization, Hydra.

As Peggy aged she began to suffer from dementia. She lived out her last days in a nursing home, sometimes believing it was World War II again.

As a teenager in Richmond, Virginia, the news of Nazi Germany's invasion of the rest of Europe shocked Peggy Carter. Determined to do something to help, she ran away from home and traveled to Paris, where she joined the French Resistance. There she became a vital spy known as Agent 13.

Peggy worked with Captain America on several occasions, and they fell in love, despite the fact that she did not know his name and had never seen him without his mask. During the liberation of Paris, the Nazis captured and interrogated Peggy. She escaped as the Allies attacked, but an artillery shell exploded close to her, giving her amnesia.

With her memory now lost, Peggy wandered aimlessly through Europe until a family friend recognized her in Belgium, and sent her back to Virginia. Learning of Cap's demise in 1945, Peggy became more reclusive. In the years that followed, she would talk to her niece, Sharon, about her wartime exploits and her romance with Captain America. Eventually, she was confined to an asylum run by corrupt psychiatrist Dr. Faustus. Faustus wanted to use Peggy to gain inside information about Cap. When Cap and Sharon Carter arrived at Faustus' asylum, they were forced to partake in a reconstruction of Peggy's final wartime battle. This helped Peggy restore her memories, and she worked with Cap and Sharon to defeat Faustus. She realized how she had aged in comparison to Cap, and she later discovered that he had fallen in love with Sharon.

After recovering, Peggy became a member of S.H.I.E.L.D., using her spy skills to help the world once again. During this time, Peggy had an on-off romance with fellow S.H.I.E.L.D. agent and World War II veteran, Gabe Jones. She went on to assist the Avengers as support staff. Eventually, she developed dementia and she was moved into a nursing home. Peggy passed away at the age of 91, and was buried in the Père Lachaise Cemetery in Paris, France.

Peggy promised Cap she would wait for him if the war ever separated them.

RIDDLE OF THE RED SKULL

In his first big adventure as Captain America, Steve Rogers and his sidekick Bucky set out to track down the mysterious killer the Red Skull.

Shortly after becoming Captain America, Steve Rogers began his fight against one of his country's most notorious enemies, the Red Skull. His first major challenge was to solve the mysterious death of Major Croy, Steve Rogers' army chief. All Cap had to go on was a dead body that was left with staring eyes and a threatening note signed by the Red Skull. While Cap went searching for clues, Bucky stumbled across the Red Skull's headquarters—and into danger! Luckily, Cap rescued him in time, but the Red Skull got away. It wasn't long until the Red Skull claimed his next victim—another military leader, General Manor. This time Cap and Bucky were able to apprehend the Red Skull, who was revealed to be George Maxon—an airplane businessman with ties to the Nazi party. In the ensuing scuffle, Maxon rolled onto a needle containing the poison he had used to kill his victims, thereby ending the riddle of the Red Skull.

BUCKY IN PERIL

Upon hearing the news of Croy's death, Cap immediately suited up, determined to bring the Red Skull to justice. Worried that the danger might be too great for his teenage sidekick, he ordered Bucky to sit this one out. Bucky, however, slipped out across the rooftops as soon as Cap was out of sight.

RESCUING BUCKY

One of the Red Skull's henchmen spotted Bucky and hauled him to the Red Skull's headquarters for his boss to pass a sentence of death. But Cap wasn't far behind. He smashed into the room and rescued Bucky. The Skull escaped through a secret doorway.

THE SKULL'S CALLING CARD

Army official Major Croy was the unlucky recipient of a written note from the Red Skull, warning him of his imminent death. The skeptical Croy ignored the threat, only to be confronted by the Red Skull in his own home. The Red Skull then murdered Croy by poisoning him with his hypnotic gaze and injecting a deadly poison from a needle. The corpse was left with staring eyes.

TRAITOR ON THE HOMEFRONT?

Cap and Bucky returned to Camp Lehigh, which soon played host to VIP military supplier George Maxon, head of the Maxon Aircraft Corporation. During a test flight, one of Maxon's planes crashed, killing its crew. Cap was horrified at the death of military personnel, but grew suspicious when Maxon showed little regret.

Another night saw another murder by the Red Skull—but this time Cap caught him in the act. Knocking the villain's mask loose with a powerful punch, Cap realized that the Red Skull was George Maxon all along. Maxon accidentally stabbed himself with a hypodermic needle filled with poison and ended his life, leaving behind a note that revealed his treasonous Nazi loyalties.

"It'll take more than you to lick this country!"

CAPTAIN AMERICA

CAP AND THE RED SKULL

The Red Skull was Captain America's most dangerous enemy—even when he was presumed dead. The villain continued to come back from the grave time after time.

The death of the Red Skull—Cap's most dangerous foe—left Steve Rogers with time on his hands to help his friend Betsy Ross with the Camp Lehigh musical. During the rehearsal, the whistle of an eerie funeral march entered the hall, and the musical's conductor, Captain Craig, suddenly collapsed dead. The Red Skull was alive! The villain had sneaked into the camp and claimed the life of the Captain by placing poison on his baton. The Red Skull was out for blood and he was determined to take down as many American military leaders as possible. The villain disappeared down the hall, ready to take his next victim, General King. But Cap and Bucky sprang into action and managed to stop the villain before he could murder King—all the while keeping their true identities concealed.

BACK FROM THE DEAD

Even his henchmen thought that the Red Skull was dead, but the villain had managed to survive his last battle with Captain America. Determined to eliminate as many members of the American military as he could, the Red Skull sneaked into the musical rehearsal at Camp Lehigh disguised as a stagehand.

CHOPIN'S FUNERAL MARCH

The Red Skull played Chopin's Funeral March on his whistle, filling the hall with creepy music, just before Captain Craig fell dead on the floor. When they heard the whistle coming from General King's room, Steve and Bucky knew that their General was in danger. The pair leapt into action as Captain America and his sidekick and burst into General King's quarters.

SURROUNDED

In General King's room, Cap and Bucky were soon surrounded by the Red Skull's henchmen. Cap was shocked to see the Red Skull standing before him— he thought he had killed him the last time they had met. Bucky and Cap got straight to work, battling the mob, but the Red Skull used the distraction to escape out of an open window, taking General King with him.

UNDER ARREST

Hearing the commotion, more army officers ran into General King's room, but they were too late—King and the Red Skull were already gone. One of the men opened a box, which contained a red skull and a note from the villain. It was addressed to Cap and said that the Red Skull had escaped with General King. The officers assumed Cap was in league with the Red Skull and were about to arrest him!

BACK TO THE GRAVE

The heroes managed to flee Camp Lehigh and hurried to a deserted dock, where the Red Skull was pushing General King onto a boat. Cap knocked the Red Skull spinning into the murky water. Cap searched the water for the villain, but he was nowhere to be seen. Bucky reminded Cap that the Red Skull couldn't swim, and they returned to Camp Lehigh, assuming the Red Skull had drowned.

DR. ABRAHAM ERSKINE

Jewish scientist Abraham Erskine dedicated his work to developing a Super-Soldier formula during World War II. The serum would transform the US Army's soldiers into perfect humans with super-strength. He achieved success with only one man—Steve Rogers—before he was shot dead by a Nazi spy.

Dr. Erskine transformed a weak Steve Rogers into the perfect human being—Captain America—with the Super-Soldier serum.

ORIGINS

Doctor Abraham Erskine was a Jewish scientist who was born and raised in Germany. His research was focused on helping humans eliminate physical defects and limitations, shaping humanity into its most perfect form.

When the Nazis came to power during the 1930s, Erskine hid his Jewish heritage. This saved him from being sent to a concentration camp. However, he was forced to take part in Project Nietzsche, the Nazi program designed to create superhumans who would become soldiers in the war. Erskine managed to get word to the Allies that he wanted to escape. The US government sent Nick Fury and Red Hargrove to rescue the scientist and bring him to America.

Once in the US—and working under the alias Josef Reinstein—Erskine began work on the Super-Soldier project, known as Operation: Rebirth. Using a Super-Soldier formula and Vita-Rays (a radiological effect used to speed up the effects of the serum), Erskine planned to transform even the weakest person into a strong soldier without physical limitations. This process could create an army of Super-Soldiers to help the war effort.

Erskine tested the serum on Steve Rogers and created Captain America. It was his first—and only—successful trial of the process. A Nazi agent named Heinz Kruger had infiltrated the top-secret installation where the project was based. As Erskine was presenting Cap to US government officials, Kruger assassinated Erskine. Paranoid about having his Operation: Rebirth secrets stolen by spies, Erskine had never written them all down in one place. The doctor's secrets died with him, leaving Captain America as the only one of his kind.

Dr. Erskine worked tirelessly to unlock the secret of the Super-Solider before the Nazis could beat him to it.

> ## "We shall call you Captain America, son! Because, like you, America shall gain the strength and will to safeguard our shores!"
>
> DR. ABRAHAM ERSKINE

Steve Rogers avenged Doctor Erskine's death right after a Nazi spy shot the doctor down.

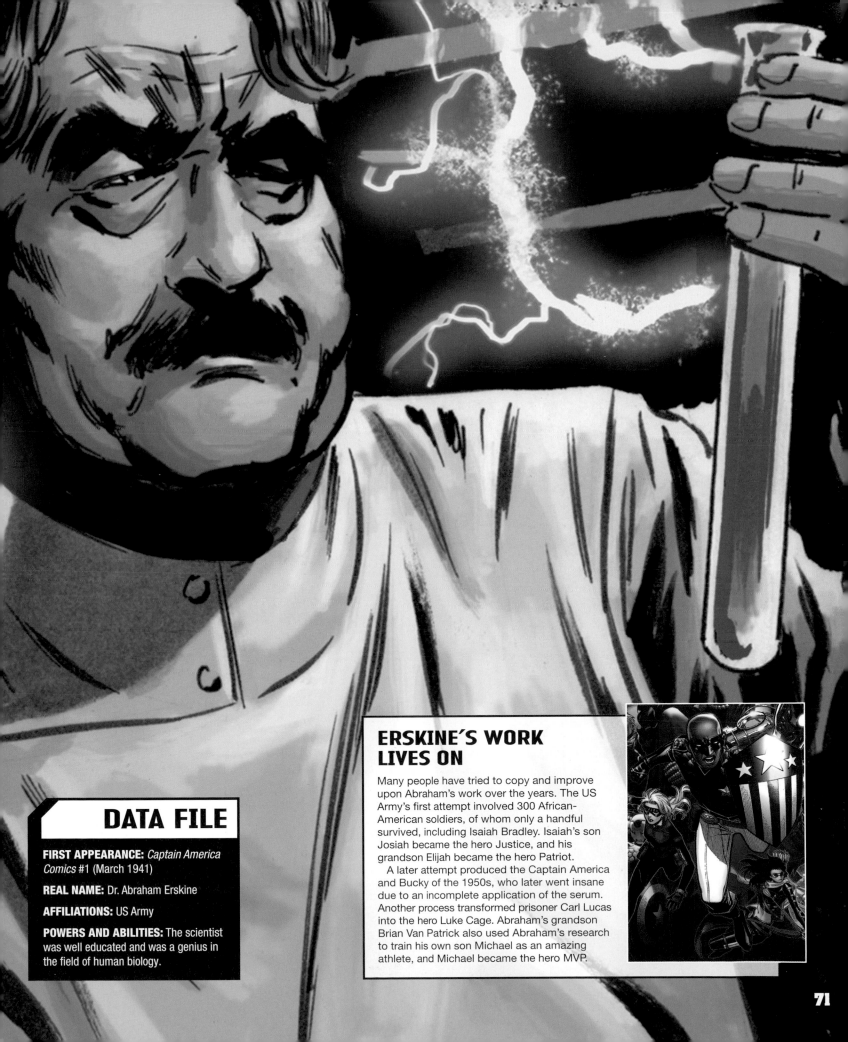

DATA FILE

FIRST APPEARANCE: *Captain America Comics* #1 (March 1941)

REAL NAME: Dr. Abraham Erskine

AFFILIATIONS: US Army

POWERS AND ABILITIES: The scientist was well educated and was a genius in the field of human biology.

ERSKINE'S WORK LIVES ON

Many people have tried to copy and improve upon Abraham's work over the years. The US Army's first attempt involved 300 African-American soldiers, of whom only a handful survived, including Isaiah Bradley. Isaiah's son Josiah became the hero Justice, and his grandson Elijah became the hero Patriot.

A later attempt produced the Captain America and Bucky of the 1950s, who later went insane due to an incomplete application of the serum. Another process transformed prisoner Carl Lucas into the hero Luke Cage. Abraham's grandson Brian Van Patrick also used Abraham's research to train his own son Michael as an amazing athlete, and Michael became the hero MVP.

CAPTAIN AMERICA COMICS #2
APRIL 1941

The US hadn't joined World War II yet, but that didn't stop Cap and Bucky's rescue mission to Europe. The heroes waged a two-man blitzkrieg on Hitler in his own backyard to save a wealthy American planning to fund the war effort against the Nazis.
Cover art: Jack Kirby

THE 19

With World War II over and the GIs back home, the Captain America of the 1950s had to deal with the rise of a brand-new foe—the Soviet Union.

The 1950s proved to be the darkest period for Captain America in many ways. With the war over, sales of *Captain America Comics* declined, and the decade had barely begun when the title was canceled with issue #75 (February 1950).

In late 1953, a new Cap and Bucky made their debut in *Young Men* #24, which also featured new Human Torch and Sub-Mariner stories. This time around, Steve Rogers was a college professor with a young student named Bucky. The popularity of these stories led to a relaunch of *Captain America Comics* with a new issue #76 in May 1954.

In these 1950s stories, Captain America and Bucky fought Communists of all stripes, including a new incarnation of the Red Skull. To make the focus crystal clear, each issue sported the supertitle "CAPTAIN AMERICA … COMMIE SMASHER!" But the renaissance proved short-lived. Sales dropped again, and *Captain America Comics* finished its run with issue #78.

OVERLEAF

Captain America Comics #77 (July 1954): This issue, midway through the title's short-lived '50s revival, sets the Communist-crushing Cap and Bucky against foes from the Soviet Union, Korea, and China.
Cover art: John Romita, Sr.

CAP FIGHTS COMMUNISM

Cap and Bucky made a brief return in the 1950s to fight Communists around the globe. It was later revealed that they weren't the real Cap and Bucky, but a pair of imposters.

FACELESS FOE

Cap and Bucky battled all sorts of Communist enemies in the 1950s, including "The Man With No Face," a Chinese spy named Philip Wing, who jumped to his apparent death when Cap and Bucky cornered him. Decades later Wing reappeared in New York City, now with powers that made him intangible, and Bucky later chased him to China.

THE CHAMPION OF SPY FIGHTERS COMES FACE TO FACE WITH THE MOST DREADED KILLER IN ALL THE RED SPY NETWORK... THE EXECUTIONER... AS CAPTAIN AMERICA FIGHTS TO PROTECT HIS COUNTRY'S TOP SECRET!

... THE EXECUTIONER!

ATOMIC SECRETS

Cap and Bucky headed west to prevent Communist spies from uncovering the secrets behind an atomic weapon that the US army was testing in the Nevada desert near Las Vegas. As well as Cap and Bucky, the spies had to contend with the mysterious spymaster known only as "The Executioner," who would instantly execute anyone who failed in their mission.

U.S. GOV PROPERT

RED SKULL'S TRAP

The Red Skull of the 1950s (Albert Malik) returned to plague Cap and Bucky once again. Disguising himself as a counter-intelligence contact, the Skull lured them into a trap and captured them. He tortured them into taking him to the location of a secret rocket atom bomb plant, but Cap fooled the villain's driver into crashing the   k, apparently killing the Skull.

ELECTRIC SHOCKER

The Soviet Union often sent its super-powered agents to deal with Cap and Bucky. A shocking villain named Electro, designed to destroy the symbol of democracy with a single touch, attacked the duo in New York City. The heroes defeated him by tricking him into standing under a waterfall as he went to recharge his powers, where he was electrocuted.

In Cap and Bucky's final adventure in the 1950s, they stopped a television repairman—who was secretly a Soviet spy—from blowing up the United Nations.

TICK TOCK TICK TOCK

CBC

JOHN ROMITA

JOHN ROMITA

THE HUMAN TORCH RETURNS

YOUNG MEN

ALL NEW STORIES!

LOOK! HE'S BACK FROM THE DEAD! IT'S THE HUMAN TORCH!

SUBMARINER AND CAPTAIN AMERICA ALSO IN THIS ISSUE

SUBMARINER

CAPTAIN AMERICA AND BUCKY

December 1953

COVER ARTIST
Carl Burgos

WRITERS
Stan Lee and Bill Everett

PENCILERS AND INKERS
Russ Heath, Carl Burgos, John Romita, Sr., Mort Lawrence, and Bill Everett

YOUNG MEN #24

"He's back from the dead! Stop him!" The Red Skull

Main characters: Captain America; Bucky Barnes; the Red Skull; the Sub-Mariner; the Human Torch **Supporting characters:** Toro; Professor Reinstein; Betty Dean **Main locations:** New York City; Berlin; Pacific Ocean; Korea; Atlantic Ocean; United Nations

BACKGROUND The 1950s was a dark time for Timely's Super Heroes. Their initial popularity had declined rapidly toward the end of the 1940s—so much so, that *Captain America Comics* had changed its name to *Captain America's Weird Tales* with issue #74 (October 1949) and was canceled the following issue, with Cap not even appearing on the final cover. In the early 1950s, the publisher tried various genres with mixed success. Horror, science fiction, westerns, romance, real-life crime, and more made it to the shelves in place of Cap and his fellow Super Heroes. By 1953, encouraged by the success his competitors were having with Super Heroes, publisher Martin Goodman thought it might be time to bring the old heroes back. He tested readers' appetites by reintroducing the big three in the *Young Men* comic. Captain America, the Sub-Mariner, and the Human Torch returned—complete with explanations of where they'd been for the last few years.

This incarnation of Cap was later retconned by Marvel to be a replacement for the "real" Cap, who'd gone missing with Bucky at the end of World War II. The Marvel Age change revealed him to be William Burnside, while "Bucky" was James Monroe, who later became the hero Nomad. This version of the Red Skull was in turn retconned to be a Communist agent. While the writer of the "Back From the Dead" strip is unknown, the artist was a young, up-and-coming penciler called John Romita, Sr., who would become one of the industry's all-time greats.

THE STORY

When the Red Skull returns and launches a daring attack on the United Nations, it's time for Captain America to come out of retirement, don his old costume, and put a stop to the Super Villain.

1

2

3

4

The Red Skull was back and planning to work with the Communists to create a vast criminal empire across the US. He showed his accomplices some old movie footage of the Skull's gang fighting Cap and Bucky—or rather, getting soundly beaten by them **(1)**. The thugs wanted reassurance that the hero was no longer around, and their boss obliged. There was no way the Red Skull would put his new plan into operation if his old nemesis were still alive. Captain America had been the only one who could defeat him in the old days, and with Cap dead, no one would be able to stop him and his Communist allies building their criminal network.

Meanwhile, it transpired that Captain America hadn't died but merely retired. His alter ego, Steve Rogers, was now a professor at the Lee School. During a history class, he told his students about how a weakling rejected by the army had gained super-powers and become Captain America. The Super-Soldier had led the fight against the Axis powers, battling spies, Nazis, and criminal masterminds, such as the Red Skull. Hearing two of his classmates ridicule Cap, a kid named Bucky started a fight with them, which was quickly stopped by Rogers **(2)**. The professor hoped a trip to New York would calm the teenager down, but on the drive into the city they heard a radio newsflash—the Red Skull was back and had attacked the United Nations, holding a number of delegates hostage until the Communists' demands were met. Luckily, Bucky had kept their old costumes safe, hidden under the backseat of Steve's car, just in case they were ever needed. The pair was soon ready to leap back into action. As they approached the United Nations building, a crowd of onlookers cheered them on, thrilled to see the heroes apparently returned from the dead.

Cap and Bucky smashed their way in, taking the villains by surprise **(3)**. The Red Skull's lackeys were no match for the two heroes and froze in fear on seeing Cap and Bucky, but the Skull himself put up more of a fight. He nearly got the better of Bucky, and was about to shoot the teen hero when Cap's shield knocked him out **(4)**. Having eliminated the threat, Cap and Bucky returned to college, where Professor Steve Rogers' students were now far more interested in the stories of Captain America's exploits. When one of the Professor's students asked whether he thought the hero was back to stay, Rogers replied that he was sure of it.

JACK MONROE

William Burnside, the Captain America of the 1950s, brought in a new young man called Jack Monroe to be his sidekick "Bucky." Jack later went on to become a Super Hero in his own right using the identity of Nomad—a title that had once belonged to his boyhood hero, the original Captain America, Steve Rogers.

ORIGINS

Jack Monroe was born on December 7, 1941—the day the Japanese Navy attacked Pearl Harbor, thrusting America into World War II. As a young boy, Jack discovered Nazi paraphernalia in his house and when he took it into school for show-and-tell, his parents were arrested for treason, along with many other parents in his hometown. Sent to a foster home, Jack took on the nickname Bucky since he idolized Cap's original sidekick.

He eventually wound up in the classroom of William Burnside, a professor so obsessed with Captain America he had changed his own name to Steve Rogers. The professor had also engineered his own version of the Super-Soldier serum after finding the formula in some Nazi files. When a new communist Red Skull attacked the United Nations building in New York City, Burnside injected himself and young Jack with his serum. William and Jack took on the identities of Captain America and Bucky, but the serum proved unstable since the two heroes hadn't received a bombardment of Vita-Rays to make it work correctly. Soon they became mentally unbalanced and the US government put them in suspended animation until a cure could be found.

Thanks to the serum, Monroe and Burnside became the 1950s Bucky and Cap.

In the modern age, the pair were inadvertantly revived by a janitor working at the facility. They went in search of the original Captain America—himself newly revived—and wound up clashing with him, having thought he was a fake.

After Jack and William were recaptured by the government, the manipulative Dr. Faustus treated their insanity. He brainwashed William to become a neo-Nazi leader called the Grand Commander. To prove his loyalty to Faustus, William shot Jack, apparently killing him. However, Jack recovered, and with his instability seemingly cured, he wanted to redeem himself. With Cap's blessing, he took on one of his Cap's earlier identities and became the Nomad.

When Jack first took on the role of Nomad, he was desperate to prove himself worthy of being Cap's partner. However, his headstrong ways could sometimes lead to him making mistakes.

"Time for Captain America to come back, Steve?" JACK MONROE

Jack once took in an abandoned young girl named Julia Winters. He made her his sidekick and nicknamed her "Bucky".

Jack was thought killed after his last adventure as Nomad, but he later reappeared as the new Super-Villain slayer, Scourge of the Underworld.

Disks recall Cap's original Nomad costume. Each 6-inch steel alloy disk can be detached and thrown to stun targets.

DATA FILE

FIRST APPEARANCE: *Young Men* #24 (December 1953)

REAL NAME: Jack Monroe

AFFILIATIONS: Captain Americas William Burnside and Steve Rogers.

POWERS AND ABILITIES: Jack's Super-Soldier serum grants him a peak human physique. He is also a trained combatant and marksman.

Combat belt features large "N" for Nomad on the buckle and pouches for storing mission-specific items.

Nomad carries guns on his missions, much to the disapproval of Cap.

THE SIDEKICK GROWS UP

Having broken free from William Burnside's influence, Jack was thrilled to work alongside the original Captain America, Steve Rogers. After some time, though, Jack struck out on his own as Nomad, roaming throughout America. He saw himself as the hero of common people down on their luck, including many homeless souls. He had sidekicks of his own for a while, including his one-time lover, Vagabond. After becoming Super Villain-killer the Scourge of the Underworld, Jack fell ill and was told he would soon lose his mind and die. He was killed by the Winter Soldier as part of a terrorist plot by the Red Skull.

THE 19

The 1960s was an era of change, when a new generation rebelled against the establishment. A man out of time, Cap embodied the nation's social and cultural tensions.

The resurgence of Super Hero comics began in November 1961 with the debut of the Fantastic Four. Spurred on by their success, editor Stan Lee decided to group some of the greatest heroes of the expanding Marvel universe into a new team, called the Avengers. An old Timely Comics character had already joined the new Marvel era when the Sub-Mariner appeared in *Fantastic Four* #4 (May 1962). Now it was Captain America's turn, with *Avengers* #4 (March 1964) introducing a man who'd been frozen in a block of ice since the final days of World War II.

Cap's rebirth in comics mirrored his rebirth in the real world. As the great wartime icon transplanted into the chaos of the 1960s, he had to figure out how to make his way in a world that had given him up for dead—and long since passed him by. Marvel's readers responded to this struggle, and Cap soon had a new series of solo stories in *Tales of Suspense*, starting with issue #59 (November 1964). Cap shared *Tales of Suspense* with Iron Man until April 1968, when he took over the title completely. Issue #100 was retitled *Captain America*.

OVERLEAF

Captain America #111 (March 1969): Cap's partner, Rick Jones, has been taken by Madame Hydra's agents. As Rick lies, gassed in the car, Cap crashes after them in hot pursuit, desperate not to lose Rick as he recently did Bucky Barnes.
Penciler: Jim Steranko
Inker: Joe Sinnot

60s

RESCUED FROM ICE

With the help of the Avengers, Cap returns from being frozen in ice, and he struggles to fit into the modern world as a man from another time.

CAP IS BACK!

After returning to modern life, Cap fought alongside the Avengers, but he soon began going on solo missions. By going on his own adventures, Cap hoped to figure out who he was in this new era—beyond being known only as the "First Avenger." Cap needed to see how America's Super-Soldier fit into post-World War II life.

THE MIND OF M.O.D.O.K.

Cap set out to rescue S.H.I.E.L.D.'s Agent 13 (Sharon Carter) from Advanced Idea Mechanics (A.I.M.)—a scientific spin-off of the villainous group Hydra, founded by Baron Strucker. After A.I.M. captured him, Cap was brought to meet their leader, known as M.O.D.O.K. (Mental Organism Designed Only for Killing). M.O.D.O.K.'s own minions rebelled against him, and Cap and Sharon managed to escape.

CAP TAKES A BREAK

Sharon Carter rejected Cap's proposal of marriage because they were committed to their jobs. So for the first time, Cap decided to turn in his uniform and shield, and he revealed his real identity to the world. After several men tried and failed to fill his boots, Cap gave in and took up his shield again.

A broken arm was one of many injuries sustained by Cap's replacements during his retirement. Each was unable to live up to Cap's abilities.

DEADLY DECEIT

Under attack by Viper and Hydra, Cap faked his death, leaving behind a costume full of bullet holes—as well as a mask of Steve Rogers, which convinced the public he'd faked the revelation of his real identity. When Hydra attacked his funeral, Cap returned to save Rick Jones (dressed as Bucky), Nick Fury, and the Avengers from their plot.

Captain America's uniform—full of bullet holes—was placed on a mannequin and laid in a coffin. A mask of Steve Rogers was also put on the dummy.

Cap speeds through the graveyard on a motorcycle at his own funeral to defeat the villainous group Hydra.

89

March 1964

WRITER
Stan Lee

COVER ARTISTS
Jack Kirby and Paul Reinman

PENCILER
Jack Kirby

INKER
George Roussos

LETTERER
Artie Simek

COLORIST
Stan Goldberg

AVENGERS #4

"Step forward Captain America! Your rightful place is here… among the Avengers!" THOR

Main characters: Captain America; Thor; Iron Man; Giant-Man; the Wasp; Namor, the Sub-Mariner **Supporting characters:** Rick Jones; the Teen Brigade; Vuk (alien, named in later stories); Bucky (flashback); Atlantean warriors **Main locations:** North Atlantic; Atlantis; Manhattan; United Nations

BACKGROUND

By the time *Avengers* #4 hit the stands in early 1964, the Marvel Age of Comics was well underway. The success of the Fantastic Four, the Amazing Spider-Man, and Iron Man had left the public hungry for more Super Hero tales. Although the first issue of the *Avengers* had been put together quickly—to replace a delayed *Daredevil* #1—it had proven to be another smash hit, and by the fourth issue it was starting to find its own identity, boosted by the addition of Captain America to the ranks. It wasn't Cap's first appearance in Marvel's new Super Hero comics. Just a few months earlier, he'd graced the cover of *Strange Tales* #114 (November 1963), fighting the Fantastic Four's Human Torch. The Cap in that issue had proven to be an imposter, but it seems the response was encouraging enough to convince Stan Lee to bring the genuine hero back.

The story set aside the Commie-smashing Captain America that had briefly appeared in the 1950s (although that version was later retconned into Marvel continuity) for the high drama of Cap as a man out of time, preserved in ice since the last days of World War II. An old-fashioned hero, with military training and patriotic all-American values, he was the leader the Avengers needed. While Cap would go on to have his own successful title in future, he quickly became identified as the Star-Spangled Avenger, one of the longest-serving members of the team.

THE STORY

No sooner have the Avengers rescued Captain America from his icy tomb than the great World War II hero is forced to step into action, joining the team to fight the menace of the Sub-Mariner.

Namor, the Sub-Mariner, was searching the sea for his lost home of Atlantis, after a battle with the Avengers. When he came across a tribe of Inuit worshipping a figure encased in ice, he chased them away and hurled the frozen figure into the ocean **(1)**. The ice cocoon soon started to melt, and the frozen figure was found by the Avengers as they traveled through the ocean in their undersea craft. As the hero regained consciousness, he cried out for his old sidekick, Bucky—only to remember that Bucky was dead.

The Wasp recognized Captain America from his costume **(2)**. Iron Man remained doubtful, but the heroes were convinced of his identity when Cap held his own in a fight against them. Cap then told them his tragic story. At the end of World War II, he and Bucky had tried to stop a stolen drone plane. Bucky managed to climb on board but Cap didn't make it in time. He fell into the sea, while Bucky was caught in the blast as the drone exploded. Cap then drifted unconscious in the ocean, becoming frozen in a state between life and death.

The Avengers landed in Manhattan to find the press waiting, eager to learn whether they had found the missing Hulk or Namor. As the photographers began to shoot, a flash turned the heroes to stone. Cap, late disembarking, noted the strange statues **(3)**, then proceeded to wander around New York, amazed at how much had changed. Rick Jones approached the hero after he checked himself into a hotel. Cap was astonished by how much Rick looked like Bucky, and agreed to help him find the missing heroes. Examining photos from the Avengers' last appearance, they realized a stranger in the crowd was holding something that looked like a gun. Cap soon located the fake reporter (with a little help from Rick's friends in the Teen Brigade), only to discover he was an alien in disguise.

The alien had crash-landed on Earth centuries before and his spaceship became trapped at the bottom of the ocean. The Sub-Mariner had promised to help free his ship if the alien turned the Avengers to stone. Now Cap convinced him that the Avengers would be able to help him—if he changed them back to flesh and blood. The alien complied and the heroes fulfilled their part of the bargain, freeing the alien ship by combining their powers and know-how.

While the alien was making last-minute underwater repairs, the Sub-Mariner and his Atlantean warriors attacked the Avengers on a nearby island. Cap leaped into action, going one-on-one with the Sub-Mariner to protect Rick Jones. After an earthquake seemed to strike the island, Namor departed, convinced his enemies had been killed in the upheaval. But it wasn't an earthquake—merely tremors caused by the alien's ship taking off. The Avengers were fine, and offered Cap a place on the team—one he gratefully accepted. Captain America was now officially an Avenger **(4)**.

SHARON CARTER

Sharon Carter grew up listening to her Aunt Peggy's tales about her missions with Captain America during World War II. Peggy's adventures inspired Sharon to become a S.H.I.E.L.D. operative, where she met Captain America. Cap and Sharon teamed up on missions and a romantic relationship blossomed.

ORIGINS

Young Sharon Carter grew up in her parents' home in Virginia, where she spent lots of time with her Aunt Peggy, who had fought with the French Resistance during World War II. During that time, Peggy had met and fallen in love with Captain America, although they were separated before the end of the war and before Cap's apparent death. Sharon loved the romance and adventure of her aunt's stories so much that she decided that she wanted to fight for her country, too. She became a S.H.I.E.L.D. operative, taking on her aunt's old codename: Agent 13. Sharon was working undercover when she first encountered Steve Rogers and fell in love with him.

Later, Sharon infiltrated neo-Nazi gang National Force. This group was organized by the Red Skull's ally Dr. Faustus and William Burnside, who had taken on the role of Captain America during the 1950s before going insane. Sharon faked her death to go deep undercover for S.H.I.E.L.D. Her death was so convincing that even S.H.I.E.L.D. presumed her dead.

Cap first encountered Sharon when he saw her transporting Inferno 42 through New York City for S.H.I.E.L.D.

Sharon returned from the dead to become the director of S.H.I.E.L.D. for a brief period. During this time, she acted as Cap's S.H.I.E.L.D. liaison officer and their romance reignited.

Later, Sharon was brainwashed by Dr. Faustus and she helped to assassinate Cap. However, the weapon Sharon used was actually a device that didn't kill Cap but froze him in time. Following his "death," Sharon learned that she was pregnant with Steve's baby, but she lost the child during a battle with Red Skull's evil daughter, Sin.

When Cap returned, Sharon proposed to him, but Cap became trapped in Dimension Z before he could answer her. Sharon found Cap in that alternate dimension where time passed faster, and sacrificed herself to save Earth from Arnim Zola's invasion. She survived and returned to Earth as an old woman, but Cap had also aged after losing the Super-Soldier serum.

Peggy sometimes suffered from amnesia, but when clear-headed she told Sharon about her adventures.

"The only thing between us and Armageddon is Captain America." SHARON CARTER

Sharon and Cap have fought side-by-side many times. She is one of his most trusted allies: He selected her to be a member of his team of Secret Avengers.

Sharon was at Cap's side when he was assassinated—but because of her brainwashing, she was unaware that she was the one who had pulled the trigger.

DIMENSION Z

Sharon was believed to have perished in the explosion in Dimension Z, but she miraculously survived. With her was Ian Zola, the boy who Steve had raised as his own during his time in Dimension Z. Sharon took over raising Ian as Steve had done, and the two became as close as mother and son. After ten years passed, Sharon was captured by Zola's Mutates. Believing that Sharon was dead, Ian managed to warn the Avengers of Zola's plot to invade Earth. During that time, Falcon found Sharon trapped in Arnim's headquarters, and with Ian's help, rescued her.

DATA FILE

FIRST APPEARANCE: *Tales of Suspense* #75 (March 1966)

REAL NAME: Sharon Carter

AFFILIATIONS: Avengers, S.H.I.E.L.D.

POWERS AND ABILITIES: Sharon is a top field agent, expert in both weaponry and martial arts. She's especially good at working as an undercover agent.

While Sharon has no powers of her own, she is a crack shot.

BECOMING CAPTAIN AMERICA

Sam has been Cap's longest-running partner—the one friend Cap trusts more than any other. When the Super-Soldier serum that gave Cap his powers and youth was drained from him, turning him into an old man, Cap chose Sam to succeed him as Captain America. When Cap was assassinated after the Superhuman Civil War, the shield passed on not to Sam but rather to Bucky. But when Cap had the chance to choose who would be his successor, Captain America chose Sam.

Sam's goggles give him infrared and telescopic vision and allow him to see 360° around him.

Sam's costume is laced with Vibranium to protect him from bullets.

This set of wings is composed of hard light and was a gift from the Black Panther.

DATA FILE

FIRST APPEARANCE: *Captain America* #117 (September 1969)

REAL NAME: Sam Wilson

AFFILIATIONS: Avengers, Heroes for Hire, Redwing, S.H.I.E.L.D.

POWERS AND ABILITIES: Sam has a telepathic link with birds, allowing him to control them and see through their eyes. This is especially strong with his falcon Redwing. Cap trained him to be a skilled fighter and a top-level aerial acrobat. His jet-powered wings enable him to fly.

THE FALCON

Sam Wilson was originally trained and controlled by the evil Red Skull, but as the skilled Super Hero "the Falcon," he was later trained by Captain America and he became his long-term adventuring partner. After Steve Rogers retired, Sam took up Cap's shield and became the new Captain America.

The Falcon's first costume was green and orange, and included a glove for his trained falcon, Redwing, to perch on.

"What kind of world will this be without a Captain America in it?"

SAM WILSON

The Falcon later changed his colors to red and white, and the Black Panther gave him a set of wings to match.

The Red Skull controlled the Falcon and used him to try to take down Cap.

Sam Wilson was born and raised in Harlem, New York City, where he became a community organizer. His father was a minister who died while trying to stop a gang fight, and later his mother was killed during a mugging, leaving Sam to raise his younger siblings—Sarah and Gideon—on his own. Despite such a hard start in life, he never lost his faith in humanity.

While he was traveling on a mission to South America, Sam's plane crashed on Exile Island in the Caribbean. He survived but encountered the Red Skull, who captured him and used a Cosmic Cube to allow Sam to communicate telepathically with his falcon, Redwing. The Red Skull trained Sam to make him the perfect crime-fighting teammate for Captain America—and a spy he could then manipulate. But the Skull's plan backfired when Sam joined with Cap to defeat him. Captain America then trained Sam in numerous fighting styles and Sam branded himself as the Falcon.

When the Red Skull found Sam, he used the Cosmic Cube to alter his mind.

Sam returned to the US where he joined Cap and the pair entered into a long partnership. A gift of jet-powered wings from the Black Panther—the king of the African nation of Wakanda—allowed the Falcon to become Cap's airborne partner.

Over the years, Sam Wilson would occasionally join the roster of the Super Hero team the Avengers. However, after Avengers member the Scarlet Witch temporarily unbalanced his mind, Sam briefly retired from being a Super Hero. He returned for a short time to support Cap's resistance to the Superhuman Registration Act during the Superhuman Civil War. Following Cap's assassination after the war, Sam registered as an official Super Hero and was assigned to protect his old neighborhood of Harlem. He later joined Heroes for Hire and returned to the Avengers.

Recently, he took over from Steve Rogers as the new Captain America, combining the Falcon's avian powers with Cap's costume and shield.

DECADES OF SCHEMES

At one point during World War II, Wolfgang came across a portal that enabled him to travel forward in time to a castle in Latveria belonging to the genius inventor and sorcerer Doctor Doom. There he stole history books from the future that told him what would happen to the Third Reich and beyond. He was not able to use the knowledge in these to alter the past, but the information he gained spurred him to consider long-term plans. Many of Wolfgang's plots from World War II have taken decades to play out, and they continue to crop up and haunt Cap.

Wolfgang is a world-class fencer, but his face was severely scarred during his training.

The Hydra symbol of a skull and six snakes is emblazoned on Wolfgang's distinctive green uniform.

DATA FILE

FIRST APPEARANCE: *Sgt. Fury and His Howling Commandos* #5 (January 1964)

REAL NAME: Wolfgang von Strucker

AFFILIATIONS: Great Wheel of the Zodiac, Hydra, Nazi Party

POWERS AND ABILITIES: Wolfgang has been infected with the Death Spore Virus, which—while being able to harm or kill most people—grants the villain superhuman durability and healing, and prevents him from aging. Wolfgang is also an expert in combat, especially with guns and swords, and he is a gifted military leader. He often uses the Satan Claw, a gauntlet that offers him strength and fires electrical shocks.

BARON VON STRUCKER

Expert military tactician and villain Wolfgang von Strucker fought for Germany in World War I and World War II. Working for Hitler's number one soldier the Red Skull, he went to Japan to create—and secretly lead—a global terrorist organization known as Hydra. From there, he set about pursuing his goal of world domination.

Posing as the Hood, von Strucker tracked down a Bucky look-alike to help him trap Cap. Unbeknownst to von Strucker, this Bucky was a robot created by evil scientist Arnim Zola.

"Hail Hydra!"
BARON WOLFGANG VON STRUCKER

ORIGINS

Two of Wolfgang's children, known as the Fenris twins, have powers when in physical contact with each other.

Cap fought Baron von Strucker, the Supreme Head of his evil organization Hydra, for decades. With Wolfgang's death at the hands of Nick Fury, his plots may have finally come to an end—although Hydra lives on.

Wolfgang von Strucker was born in the late 1800s to a family of Prussian nobles. He fought on the side of Germany during World War I, and he did the same again during World War II, joining the Nazi Party. He became commander of the famed Death's Head Squadron and faced off many times against US Army Sergeant Nick Fury and his unit of oddball soldiers the Howling Commandos. Wolfgang also battled Captain America during World War II, as well as Cap's Super Hero team the Invaders. He worked alongside Super Villain the Red Skull to further the Nazi war effort, including trying to find the legendary Hammer of Skadi.

When it seemed clear Germany would lose the war, Wolfgang traveled to Japan to join forces with the criminal organization known as the Hand. He formed a subversive organization that would eventually become the global terrorist powerhouse named Hydra.

Wolfgang's desire for worldwide domination led him to clash with Captain America and the espionage agency S.H.I.E.L.D. on many occasions. Cap's wartime pal Nick Fury—working as a S.H.I.E.L.D. operative—discovered Wolfgang's plan to use Hydra technology to develop a device known as the Overkill Horn that would detonate all the nuclear bombs around the globe. Soon after, Nick found out about plans to release a bio-engineered Death Spore bomb which would release a plague onto the people of Earth. Fortunately, Nick was able to foil both evil plans just in time.

Wolfgang fathered several children, including a son, Werner, and twins called Andreas and Andrea, who were known as the Fenris twins. He has died more than once, but has been able to continue his work through the use of clones, resurrection, and Life Model Decoys.

Wolfgang went to Antarctica to retrieve the Hammer of Skadi for the Red Skull.

97

CAPTAIN AMERICA #111

"Hail Hydra! This time, Captain America shall not escape!" Hydra agent

Main characters: Captain America; Rick Jones; Madame Hydra **Supporting characters:** Hydra agents; Mankiller robot **Main locations:** New York City; Avengers Mansion

BACKGROUND
Published at the end of the 1960s, *Captain America* #111 captured not just the themes, but also the unmistakable style of an era. Building on the foundations laid by Kirby, Ditko, Romita, and Buscema, newer artists, such as Jim Steranko and Neal Adams, ensured that Marvel's visuals were bang up-to-date and reflected the art and pop culture of the Swinging Sixties. Before his short run on *Captain America*, Jim Steranko had already illustrated Nick Fury's adventures for Marvel, his famously innovative work introducing elements of modern art—surrealism, Op Art, psychedelia—to the page. Steranko was also a musician, graphic designer, and magician—and you can see how his life outside of comics seeped into his work. With Marvel maestro Stan Lee on scripts, the pair created a short run of fantastic Cap adventures. Steranko illustrated only three issues but they remain some of Cap's best comics.

Marvel Comics enjoyed a constant flow of new concepts throughout the 1960s, from the birth of the first Super Hero team—the Fantastic Four—to Spider-Man's dramatic love life, as well as some truly malevolent villains. This period also saw the return of older heroes such as Cap and the Sub-Mariner, who were re-invented for a new generation of readers.

Rick Jones, the teenage friend of the Incredible Hulk, had recently taken on the role of Bucky, and was plagued by doubts about his abilities. At the same time, a resurgent Hydra had gained a new leader—Madame Hydra—just as Cap had revealed his secret identity to the world, making him an easier target than ever before.

March 1969

COVER ARTIST
Jim Steranko

WRITER
Stan Lee

PENCILER
Jim Steranko

INKER
Joe Sinnott

LETTERER
Sam Rosen

COLORIST
Jim Steranko

THE STORY

As Rick Jones tries to prove himself worthy of his role as the new Bucky, Captain America finds himself vulnerable to attack when Hydra's boss, Madame Hydra, lays a deadly trap for the Star-Spangled Avenger.

Steve Rogers had arranged to meet S.H.I.E.L.D. boss Nick Fury at the penny arcade in an amusement park. While waiting, Steve used a fortune-telling machine that gave him the grim prediction, "tomorrow you live… tonight I die!" **(1)**. As Steve worried that Nick was late, he caught sight of assassins approaching. Now that the world knew his identity, he had become easy prey. Too late, Steve realized that Nick hadn't arranged the meeting—it was a trap set by the criminal organization Hydra. As the Hydra agents attacked, Steve slipped into his costume, avoiding their bullets. Cap was after Hydra's leader, Madame Hydra, but the agents were prepared to die rather than reveal her whereabouts. After the defeated Hydra team had returned to base, Madame Hydra **(2)** killed an agent by testing a hallucinogenic drug on him—a warning that failure would not be tolerated—and sent Hydra agents out again to destroy Captain America.

Later, at Avengers Mansion, Cap showed Rick Jones footage of Bucky in action and demonstrated how to use acrobatics in combat. But instead of inspiring Rick, this only made him feel more insecure—he could never live up to the legendary Bucky. After Rick quit training for the day, he spotted a letter addressed to Cap, marked urgent. Opening the envelope, Rick was knocked unconscious by the hallucinogenic gas inside, which gave him terrifying visions of Bucky's death and his own inability to replace him **(3)**. When Hydra agents arrived to collect their victim, they realized it wasn't Cap, but took Rick anyway. Cap arrived moments later, and hurled himself through the mansion's windows in an attempt to rescue Rick. Cap managed to capture one agent, who was then killed by his comrades as they fled. Back at Hydra's base, Madame Hydra ordered her agents to dispose of Rick and set another trap for Cap at the penny arcade. Luckily, Rick was only feigning unconsciousness, and soon managed to escape.

Cap was attacked by one of the group's Mankiller robots while searching for clues to Hydra's whereabouts at the arcade. After a ferocious battle, Cap managed to make it to the arcade's roof, which gave him more space to fight. When the robot tried to fire missiles at Cap from its chest, Cap used his shield and the missiles rebounded to explode inside the robot **(4)**. Now he was trapped on the roof, surrounded by Hydra agents. Bucky shouted a warning and Cap leaped into the water around the docks, pursued by a storm of bullets. In the aftermath, the police could find only Cap's costume in the water—riddled with bullet holes—and a face mask that resembled Steve Rogers. This seemed to prove that Captain America wasn't Steve Rogers after all, his alter ego a mystery once more.

BURYING ZEMO

When Captain America discovered Zemo's crushed corpse, he said, "You can rest easier now, Bucky—wherever you may be. Your death has been avenged!" Together with Rick, Cap gave the Baron a decent burial in the South American jungle. Then they turned their attentions to getting back to the Avengers.

THE OLD ORDER CHANGETH!

When the founding members of the Super Hero team the Avengers decided they needed a break, they had to find replacements and a new hero to lead them.

Captain America had flown to South America to rescue his crime-fighting partner Rick Jones from Nazi scientist Baron Heinrich Zemo—the man who had almost killed Cap and Bucky back in 1945. While attacking Cap, Zemo's shot with his disintegrator pistol went wild and caused an avalanche that killed the villain. Cap and Rick buried Zemo and set out for Manhattan.

Meanwhile, the rest of the Avengers team had been left to fight Zemo's villainous group the Masters of Evil. After they triumphed, Thor left for Asgard for a trial of the gods that saw him being pitted against his adopted brother, Loki. The remaining Avengers confessed to each other that they needed a break from the team.

After an exhaustive hunt, founding Avengers members Iron Man, Giant-Man, and the Wasp chose Hawkeye, Scarlet Witch, and Quicksilver to replace them. Cap and Rick arrived at Avengers Mansion where they met the new line-up and Iron Man handed over leadership to Cap.

TIME TO DISBAND?

With Cap and Thor gone and the Masters of Evil defeated, Giant-Man, Wasp, and Iron Man had the first quiet moment to themselves in a while. The Wasp suggested that they take a break. They might have disbanded permanently then and there if Hawkeye hadn't broken into the Avengers Mansion at that same moment to petition for membership.

CAP'S BACK

Having accepted Hawkeye onto the team, the Avengers interviewed new applicants. Although the Sub-Mariner refused to join, brother and sister duo Quicksilver and Scarlet Witch applied. Cap and Rick arrived just as the super-powered siblings were being inducted. With Iron Man taking a break, Cap agreed to lead the new line-up of Avengers.

INTRODUCING...

All three of the new Avengers had started out as criminals. Hawkeye had fought Iron Man alongside the Black Widow, and Scarlet Witch and Quicksilver had been part of the Brotherhood of Evil Mutants. The Avengers vetted and vouched for each of them, though, and they became part of Cap's brand-new Avengers team.

RETURN OF THE RED SKULL

Captain America leapt into action when he spotted suspicious soldiers on the streets of New York. Unfortunately, no one else could see them, not even a sympathetic policeman. The truth was the Red Skull was employing a hypnotic device in a bid to make Cap doubt his own sanity.

THE RED SKULL LIVES

Captain America's nemesis—the Red Skull— had returned. His mission was to take over the universe using the all-powerful Cosmic Cube.

Cap's most vile villain was back, and more powerful than ever! Both Captain America and the Red Skull were legacies of World War II, brought out of suspended animation to continue their battle. With the debut of the all-new Cosmic Cube—believed to be the product of the sinister organization A.I.M. (Advanced Idea Mechanics)—the Red Skull would come close to gaining dominance over the world—and after that, even the universe. Luckily, Cap was on the case and tracked the Cosmic Cube to a remote island where he faced the Red Skull. In the ensuing battle that saw Cap confront a man made from sand, Cap realized that the day could not be won with muscle, but with cunning.

The Red Skull gained power over all reality with the Cosmic Cube, an object that turned its wielder into a god. Intoxicated with visions of conquering Earth and sending a fleet of starships to unite the galaxy under his rule, the Red Skull still viewed Captain America's humiliation as his greatest triumph.

Cap was ready for the Skull's hypnotic tricks next time, but the crash of an A.I.M. aircraft in the harbor keyed Cap in to the existence of the Cosmic Cube. He realized what it would mean for the world if the Red Skull unleashed the full extent of the Cube's powers.

WIELDING THE COSMIC CUBE

Tracking the Red Skull to a remote island base, Cap discovered that he was too late to stop his enemy from claiming control of the Cosmic Cube. The Red Skull comprehended the cosmic mastery he now possessed. The Red Skull gloated as he reveled in fantasies of grinding the world and the entirety of interstellar space under his boot heel. As a demonstration of his new gifts, he formed a humanoid golem from the sand.

"I'm the Red Skull— the master of the world! I must rule!"

THE RED SKULL

GAINING THE UPPER HAND

Cap realized he had to outwit his evil opponent. Appealing to the Red Skull's vanity, he prostrated himself and offered his services as a devoted knight. The ruse provided the opening Cap needed to knock the Cosmic Cube from the Red Skull's hand. The Red Skull tried to retrieve his prize and the island was torn to pieces. In the end, both the Red Skull and the Cosmic Cube sank beneath the waves.

THE
19

The 1970s was a time of turmoil, both for Captain America and the United States. But they would weather the many changes and emerge all the stronger for it.

In 1970, Cap's co-creator Jack Kirby left Marvel for a few years, putting the hero in the hands of new writers and artists keen to tackle fresh and topical stories. These included a tale in which the leader of the subversive Secret Empire was revealed to be a high-ranking member of the US government. Rather than be captured, Number One committed suicide. Although his face was never revealed, *Captain America* #175 (July 1974) implied that Number One was none other than President Richard Nixon, who was embroiled in the Watergate scandal and would resign office later that year.

Disillusioned by the subsequent cover-up, Steve Rogers quit, deciding that he could no longer stomach being a symbol of such a government. He would return as Captain America several issues later, vowing to represent the ideals of the American people rather than their politicians, which put him back in costume in time to celebrate the US bicentennial of 1976.

The nature of Cap's adventures would change in other ways, too. From February 1971 to June 1978, Cap shared the title with best pal Sam Wilson, as the comic was renamed *Captain America and the Falcon*.

OVERLEAF

Captain America #134 (February 1971): Captain America and the Falcon share a comic's title for the first time when Sam's nephew gets involved with the Stone-Face gang in Harlem. Cover art: Herb Trimpe, Marie Severin, John Romita, Sr., Morrie Kuramoto

70s

TURBULENT TIMES

Cap's faith in his role and the country he served has been shaken to the core during events such as these. Nonetheless, he has always rallied to America's call.

THE LEADER REVEALED

Captain America chased the leader of a criminal enterprise known as the Secret Empire into the White House and unmasked him, only to recoil at discovering the man's true identity. The man was rumored to be the President of America himself! Rather than be captured, the villain killed himself. The US government covered up the affair by using a body double and Cap became so disillusioned that he gave up the role of Captain America.

NOMAD RISES

After giving up the role of Cap, Steve Rogers could not bring himself to stay out of the action. In order to declare his independence from the government, Steve fashioned himself a new costume and identity, and went by the name of Nomad. In Nomad's first adventure, he took on the Super Villain Viper and her criminal business enterprise, the Serpent Squad.

GIANT PROBLEMS

Cap discovered that an old enemy, Nazi scientist-turned-spy Lyle Dekker, had survived World War II and had set up a base in Newfoundland. There, he made a 12-foot replica of Cap! Dekker then proceeded to transfer his own mind into this giant creation—which he called the Ameridroid. Cap soundly defeated his huge doppelganger.

NO SUBSTITUTE

Following the Secret Empire scandal, Steve Rogers gave up being Captain America. His successor was young Roscoe Simons, with the Falcon as his partner. He didn't last long in the role, however. When the Red Skull discovered that Roscoe wasn't the original Cap, he tortured and killed him out of spite. Steve donned Cap's costume once again and went after his archenemy, the Red Skull.

August 1974

COVER ARTIST
John Romita, Sr.

WRITER
Steve Englehart

PENCILER
Sal Buscema

INKER
Vince Colletta

LETTERER
Artie Simek

COLORIST
Linda Lessman

CAPTAIN AMERICA #176

"Blast it! I'm no legend! I'm a man!" STEVE ROGERS

Main characters: Captain America; Thor; Iron Man; Vision; Falcon; Peggy Carter; Sharon Carter **Supporting characters:** The Red Skull; Bucky Barnes; Professor Reinstein; Kang; Mole Man; M.O.D.O.K.; Jarvis
Main locations: New York City; Avengers Mansion

BACKGROUND
An epilogue to one of Captain America's greatest sagas—"The Secret Empire"—*Captain America* #176 was released at the height of the Watergate scandal, a few months before Nixon's resignation in August 1974 (comics were published three months ahead of their cover date). The previous issue's shocking climax had revealed the head of the underground organization to be a high-ranking US government official (in a later interview, writer Steve Englehart admitted that he wrote the leader as Nixon, but censored himself at the last moment). Echoing the soul-searching that many Americans experienced as their President's corruption was uncovered, Steve Rogers contemplated whether to quit his role as the Star-Spangled Avenger.

Englehart's script provided a fresh take on the hero's origins, as Cap looks back over his career—interestingly, the scientist behind the Super-Soldier serum was again called Professor Reinstein (this name was later retconned to be a code name for Dr. Erskine).

Sharon Carter was portrayed here as Peggy Carter's younger sister. While that was still viable in 1973, by the time of Ed Brubaker's run on the title in 2005 (which launched *Captain America* Vol. 5), Marvel's sliding timescale meant Sharon had become Peggy's niece.

With its dramatic cover art by John Romita, Sr., this key issue saw Steve Rogers make the fateful decision to turn his back on Captain America, sickened by the actions of a government he once trusted. It was a powerful message during troubled times.

THE STORY

A disillusioned Steve Rogers contemplates quitting his role as Captain America and turns to his closest friends—as well as his allies in the Avengers—for advice, before making his life-changing decision.

"Captain America must die…" were the words uttered by Steve Rogers **(1)**, as he considered his future in the wake of the Secret Empire's defeat. The shady organization had started as an offshoot of Hydra but had evolved into a covert group with members in positions of power across the country—including in the White House itself. While he had proven his innocence after being framed for murder by the Secret Empire, the shocking suicide of its leader, Number One—and the knowledge that Number One was a high-ranking politician, signalling corruption at the heart of the United States—had left Steve shaken to the core.

Revisiting his past **(2)**, Steve recalled how patriotic he had once been, how he had kept trying to join the army despite being told he was too frail. It was this determination that brought him to the attention of Professor Reinstein, who transformed him from a weakling into the world's first and only Super-Soldier, in 1941. Since then, he had fought the Nazis alongside Bucky, become frozen in ice—only to find himself alive again, decades later—and joined the Avengers. He had teamed up with Falcon and fallen in love with Sharon Carter.

As Cap contemplated his life, on the roof of Avengers Mansion, his fellow heroes came to offer advice. Thor urged him to continue, telling him that there was nothing more glorious than a just battle. Iron Man reminded Cap how lucky they were to be heroes, and pointed out how many lives Captain America had saved. But Cap was having none of it. If the people genuinely loved him as a hero, why had they turned on him so quickly when the Secret Empire had manipulated the media to portray Captain America as a vigilante?

As they continued to talk inside, Falcon burst in **(3)**, angry at Cap for not telling him what he was considering. He explained to his friend how much difference Cap had made to his own life, by training Sam Wilson to become the Falcon and taking him on as his partner. For her turn, Peggy Carter insisted that Steve was more than just a Super Hero. He was, she said, the true embodiment of the American dream. Vision almost had the last word. The android Avenger told Cap to ask himself if he could really turn away from a life of adventure. Finally, it was down to Sharon Carter. She promised Steve that she would love him no matter what—she had fallen in love with the man behind the mask, and not the hero it represented.

Alone at last, Cap came to his fateful decision **(4)**. Although he had been created to serve the government of the United States, now he realized that the government served only itself, not the people. "I'm the one who's seen everything Captain America fought for become a cynical sham!" he proclaimed, telling the other Avengers that he was done with life as a hero. Captain America was dead.

ARNIM ZOLA

A pioneer in both robotics and genetics, Nazi scientist Arnim Zola helped not only Adolf Hitler, but also the Red Skull and Baron Zemo in their attempts to conquer the world. However, despite gaining near-immortality by transferring his mind into a robotic body, Arnim has not been able to defeat Captain America.

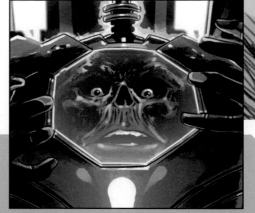

For a while, the Red Skull's mind was housed in one of Zola's spare robotic bodies.

ORIGINS

Swiss scientist Arnim Zola made huge advances in his research into genetics after stumbling across mysterious papers belonging to his ancestors. These documents had originated long ago from a branch of humanity known as the Deviants, and contained secrets of genetic engineering that were far in advance of modern-day technology. Undeterred by ethics, Arnim found himself in league with the Nazi Party, where he found favor with Adolf Hitler and partnered up with Hitler's protégé, the Red Skull. He discovered a way to place his own mind into a robotic form of his own construction, thereby replacing his frail body with something more durable. Arnim projected an image of his face onto a screen in the center of his chest. He placed an ESP (Extra Sensory Perception) Box on top of his body and attached it to his central nervous system—allowing him mental control over his creations.

A world-leading biochemist, Arnim was closely associated with the Nazi party.

In need of funds to continue his research, Arnim struck a deal with Hitler, transferring Hitler's mind into a cloned body in exchange for his patronage. One of these clones would go on to become the Hate-Monger, a villain who would plague the Fantastic Four and Captain America. Arnim also gave the Red Skull the ability to put himself into suspended animation so he could survive the end of World War II. In addition, he created size-changing androids for fellow Nazi scientist Baron Helmut Zemo that could grow from the size of dolls to that of an adult human.

After the war, Arnim helped Baron Wolfgang von Strucker build the criminal organization Hydra. Arnim created a robotic body for the Supreme Hydra, making him effectively ageless and enabling him to patiently wait for many of his long-term schemes to bear fruit.

When the Red Skull came out of suspended animation he brought new funds and purpose to Arnim's research. Arnim made a clone of Cap for the Red Skull to project his mind into. This was not to last.

> ### "I am the master! The master of all I create!" ARNIM ZOLA

Zola created a son for himself in Dimension Z, but Cap rescued the child as an infant and adopted him as his own son, Ian Rogers.

Zola also created a daughter named Jet Black, whom he raised to adulthood. When Jet discovered his evil plans, though, she betrayed him.

DATA FILE

FIRST APPEARANCE: *Captain America* #208 (April 1977)

REAL NAME: Arnim Zola

AFFILIATIONS: Baron Helmut Zemo, Baron von Strucker, Hydra, Ian Rogers, Jet Black, Nazi Party, the Red Skull

POWERS AND ABILITIES: Arnim is a genius who specializes in biochemistry, cloning, genetics, and robotics. When in a robotic body, he has superhuman durability and strength. He can also control his genetic creations via telepathy and can transfer his mind into them when necessary.

Zola's robotic body has an ESP Box atop its shoulders. This allows him to control his creations by means of telepathy.

Zola built a robotic body for himself and projected his mind into it.

Zola's face is actually an image generated on a screen affixed to his chest. In later models, he uses a holographic display.

DIMENSION Z

Arnim discovered an alternate reality—named Dimension Z—in which time flowed much faster than in the regular world. Effectively immortal as a robot, Arnim retreated there to build an army of mutates—creatures with a genetic mutation— and even a family for himself. Experiments that took years to bear fruit in Dimension Z only took minutes in the real world, giving him ample time to found a city called Zolandia and expand his empire. Cap stumbled into Dimension Z where he rescued Arnim's infant son Ian, raising him as his own, and led a rebellion of the native Phrox against Arnim that nearly destroyed the place.

HEROES AND VILLAINS

Helmut gathered his own version of the Masters of Evil and fought Cap and the Avengers many times. When the Avengers disappeared after a battle with the Super Villain Onslaught, Helmut transformed his team into the Thunderbolts, and they pretended to be heroes. Helmut took up the identity of Citizen V, a World War II hero that his father had murdered. When Helmut was ready to make his move to take over the world, the rest of the Thunderbolts resisted. They had come to enjoy being heroes and fought against Helmut to keep the world safe and to remain as heroes. To appease them, Helmut agreed, but he really set his sights on saving the world by ruling it.

DATA FILE

FIRST APPEARANCE: *Captain America* #168 (December 1973)

REAL NAME: Helmut Zemo

AFFILIATIONS: Hydra, Masters of Evil, Redeemers, Thunderbolts, V-Battalion

POWERS AND ABILITIES: Helmut is a scientist and tactician. He's also an expert combatant, particularly proficient with swords and guns. Helmut reinvented his father's death ray (a superweapon from World War II) and permanent glue ("Adhesive X"). Helmut's headband protects him against telepathic powers, and he uses his father's invention, a serum named Compound X, to keep himself young.

Helmut incorporated circuitry into his headband to protect his mind from psychic assault.

Following his accident with Adhesive X, Helmut chooses to wear a purple mask in honor of his father.

Helmut's costume resembles that of his father, including his use of purple, his fur mantle, and his golden belt.

BARON HELMUT ZEMO

The son of a scientist and prominent Nazi supporter, Helmut Zemo spent much of his life trying to live up to his father Heinrich's legacy. He also attempted to avenge Heinrich's death by eliminating Captain America. Although Zemo tried his hand at being a hero, his twisted motives always brought him down.

Before his face became permanently disfigured, Baron Helmut Zemo called himself the Phoenix.

"Guide my hand father, as I avenge your death!"

BARON HELMUT ZEMO

Helmut's father, Heinrich Zemo, was a remarkable scientist, a prominent member of the Nazi Party, and a mortal foe of Captain America.

Zemo's group the Masters of Evil included the Beetle, Fixer, Goliath, Moonstone, and Screaming Mimi. This incarnation went on to form the Thunderbolts.

Helmut Zemo was the son of Baron Heinrich Zemo—a Nazi scientist who designed super-weapons for the Reich during World War II, including an indissoluble glue known as "Adhesive X," which was created to immobilize Allied troops. However, Captain America broke into Heinrich's lab before it could be used. In the ensuing fight, Cap's shield broke the vat of glue, which splattered onto Heinrich's face and permanently affixed his mask to his head. He became obsessed with trying to destroy Captain America, but was ultimately crushed in a landslide during a battle with Cap.

The Baron's son, Helmut, dedicated his life to avenging his father's death. Calling himself the Phoenix, Helmut attempted to drown Cap in a boiling vat of Adhesive X. The liquid splashed onto Helmut's skin, permanently disfiguring his face. He subsequently wore a mask.

Helmut organized a new incarnation of a group of Super Villains known as the Masters of Evil—his father had formed the original group—and battled the Avengers. Later, Zemo called himself Citizen V and he transformed the Masters of Evil into a group of Super Heroes called the Thunderbolts. As Citizen V, Helmut Zemo pretended to be a Super Hero but secretly he attempted to take over the world. The Thunderbolts thwarted him and knocked him into a time vortex. When Zemo returned, he had a change of heart and dedicated himself to helping the world. However, he was embittered by Captain America's attempts to cover up crimes committed by the Winter Soldier—crimes that had been committed under mind control. Zemo took it upon himself to expose those crimes before turning his attention to Hawkeye, who had taken control of the Thunderbolts from him.

Helmut Zemo tried to avenge his father Heinrich Zemo's death by killing Cap.

CAPTAIN AMERICA #200
AUGUST 1976

The 200th issue of Captain America
coincided with the 200th anniversary
of the birth of the United States. While
readers celebrated the signing of the
Declaration of Independence, Cap and
Falcon raced to save the United States
from the Madbomb.
Cover art: Jack Kirby and Frank Giacoia

SECRET ORIGINS

Captain America had always been Steve Rogers—hadn't he? But if Cap was frozen in ice at the end of World War II, what did that mean for Cap and Bucky's adventures during the late 1940s and early 1950s?

Captain America and Bucky were back in action—or at least that's what it looked like when the Falcon encountered the pair on the streets of Harlem. However, these weren't androids or clones, but something far more dangerous. William Burnside and Jack Monroe had adventured as Captain America and Bucky during a brief postwar period before disappearing from the public eye. Now they had returned, but their actions were angry and violent. The true Captain America and his new partner Falcon had to defeat their doppelgangers, demonstrating the superiority of multicultural cooperation over their enemies' narrow political views.

FALCON ON THE CASE

While patrolling his home turf in New York City's Harlem, the Falcon saw what appeared to be Captain America beating up helpless victims. Knowing that this couldn't be Steve Rogers, Falcon intervened—only to be captured by the imposter and his sidekick, Bucky. Kept prisoner inside a warehouse, the Falcon refused to give up the location of the real Captain America. Falcon's friends from the neighborhood freed him, giving the hero just enough time to learn that Steve Rogers was vacationing on a remote island with his girlfriend, S.H.I.E.L.D. agent Sharon Carter.

SNEAK ATTACK

The imposters beat Falcon to the vacation spot, ambushing Rogers and Carter on the beach and adding the Falcon to their collection of prisoners when he arrived too late to warn them. With their three captives restrained in the cargo hold, the false Cap and Bucky piloted their seaplane toward Miami.

TWISTED HISTORY

During the voyage, William Burnside and Jack Monroe revealed their identities as the Communist-smashing Cap and Bucky of the 1950s. The prisoners escaped when the seaplane touched down at the Miami docks, and Burnside and Monroe slipped away, vowing to settle things once and for all at Miami's Torch of Friendship monument.

The fake Captain America, William Burnside, saw his uniform ripped to shreds and his shield crumple when he entered into combat with the genuine article. This cosmetic damage symbolized the difference between Cap's true patriotism and the hollow, reactionary ideology of Burnside's anti-Communism.

CAP VS. CAP

Sharon and Falcon took care of Bucky, allowing Captain America to battle Burnside one-on-one. Against the backdrop of the memorial, the two traded blows and verbal jabs. When Burnside finally understood that his opponent was the genuine World War II hero, he lost his grip on reality. Cap took him down and recommended that both imposters received medical treatment. Cap then vowed to "go back to fighting for a better America."

RETURN OF THE ARISTOCRACY

William Taurey used his wealth to assemble a mercenary army, the "Royalist Forces of America." Obsessed with his ancestor's death at the hands of Captain Steven Rogers 200 years ago, Taurey sought to re-establish an aristocracy in the United States on the day of the Bicentennial, and to restore his family's honor by defeating Rogers' only living descendant, Captain America.

THE KILL-DERBY

A series of clues led Cap and Falcon to an underground lair in the middle of the desert. A member of Taurey's Elite—Cheer Chadwick—took a liking to the pair, giving them a tour of the facility. For Cheer's amusement, Cap and Falcon were placed in a "Kill-Derby" to battle other combatants to the death. Luckily, an attack on the complex by the US military provided the distraction that the heroes needed to make their escape.

TAKING DOWN THE MADBOMB

The endgame against the Royalists was a two-pronged attack. While Captain America infiltrated the Taurey estate, the Falcon and a squad of S.H.I.E.L.D. agents stormed a building in downtown Philadelphia that housed the "Big Daddy" Madbomb.

MADBOMB

Villains threatened to destroy America's bicentennial celebrations, so Captain America and the Falcon joined forces once again to keep the country safe.

The Madbomb was a superweapon that emitted sonic waves, driving its victims into a bloodthirsty rage. As Captain America and his partner the Falcon soon discovered, previous outbreaks of Madbomb fury were only test runs for the unveiling of "Big Daddy"—a missile-sized weapon to be triggered on July 4, 1976. On that day, America's Bicentennial, the nation's citizens would become mindless animals who would attack one another—unless Cap could stop the countdown.

Cap and the Falcon embarked on a journey that took them into the twisted expanse of a secret mountain HQ. It was here that William Taurey, the wealthy descendant of British aristocrats, was planning to engineer a social takeover that would put the elite in charge of America once more. Taurey bore a grudge over his ancestor's loss to Colonial soldier Steven Rogers in a duel during the Revolutionary War. Luckily, Captain America foiled Taurey's takeover attempt, and the Falcon successfully deactivated the giant bomb. America was safe once again.

A NATION IS SAVED

Captain America confronted William Taurey, having overheard his desire for a duel with Steve Rogers. Both men took up their duelling pistols, but the cowardly Taurey lost his nerve, just as Cap suspected he would. Meanwhile, Falcon overloaded the Madbomb, which tore itself apart. Upon [...]ng the news, a relieved Cap observed, "The nation stands."

"It took 200 years, Falcon. But this country has grown up!"

CAPTAIN AMERICA

Captain America and the Falcon tackled conspiracies and futuristic threats while working the Madbomb case. The Bicentennial event presented a ticking-clock scenario, requiring the two heroes to infiltrate a hidden headquarters and come up with a plan to save the nation from descending into crazed chaos.

Cap's work with the Avengers continued strong through the 1980s, but Steve Rogers quit as Captain America for a while, to avoid becoming a pawn of the government.

With the Vietnam War in the rear-view mirror and the dissolution of the Soviet Union on the horizon, the 1980s proved fertile ground for Captain America. Cap turned down the chance to run for President in 1980, disappointing many supporters—including his fellow Avengers. Before long, the Iran-Contra scandal had wrecked President Reagan's attempts to rebuild confidence in the government after Watergate, and the national mood was reflected in Cap's storylines, with new villains such as Flag-Smasher appearing, after Mark Gruenwald took over writing duties.

A reformed enemy fought alongside Cap for a while, adopting one of Steve's former identities, the Nomad. Then, once again, Steve Rogers hung up his shield, taking on a new identity and letting another man—John Walker, the Super-Patriot—serve in his place. Steve would not resume his role as Captain America for well over a year.

Meanwhile, many of Cap's adventures with the Avengers and other heroes ignored earthly politics entirely and took him to far-flung planets. There he would battle against superhumans and lead the fight against the mysterious cosmic entity known as the Beyonder.

OVERLEAF

Captain America #321 (September 1986): Cap is forced to shoot in order to rescue the hostages of a hijacked plane from the villain Flag-Smasher and his terrorist group, Ultimatum.
Cover art: Mike Zeck, John Beatty

CAPTAIN OF WHAT?

Cap always fought the good fight, but he sometimes struggled with the idea of who or what he was standing up for. In the end, Cap realized he was fighting for the ideals of what America could be at its best.

CAP FOR PRESIDENT?

After stopping a hostage-taker at the convention of the New Populist Party —a small political organization—Cap was asked to run for President of the United States on the New Populist Party ticket. After some soul-searching, and fielding offers from the Democratic and Republican parties, Cap declined the offer, believing he could do more good as a hero than as President.

DEADLY GAME

An Elder of the Universe—known as the Grandmaster—liked playing games and so he challenged Death to a contest over the life of the Collector, one of his fellow Elders who had been murdered. To play out their game, they kidnapped Earth's Super Heroes and selected teams of champions. Cap was chosen for the Grandmaster's team, which eventually won the competition, allowing the Collector to be brought back to life. Death stipulated that for the Collector to live, the Grandmaster would have to take his place in death. The Grandmaster agreed.

NEW CAP, NEW ERA

When Steve Rogers gave up being Captain America, the Presidential committee that claimed power over his costume, shield, and identity gave them all to someone else. John Walker— formerly the hero Super-Patriot—was their choice, along with his pal Lemar Hoskins, who became the new Bucky. A while later, Hoskins changed his codename to Battlestar.

BATTLE PLANET

An infinitely powerful being called the Beyonder summoned Earth's greatest heroes and villains to a planet of his own creation—Battleworld—and pitted them against each other so he could study their interactions. Cap guided the heroes and led them on a final assault against Doctor Doom who had stolen the Beyonder's power. Doom lost, the Beyonder regained his power, and they all left Battleworld.

RISE OF THE CAPTAIN

Replaced by John Walker as Captain America, Steve Rogers gave up being a hero for a while. His old crime-fighting partners—the Falcon, Nomad, and D-Man—tracked him down to convince him to take up a new role as The Captain. D-Man gave him a red, white, and black costume, and later on, Tony Stark (aka Iron Man) gave him a new shield made of Adamantium.

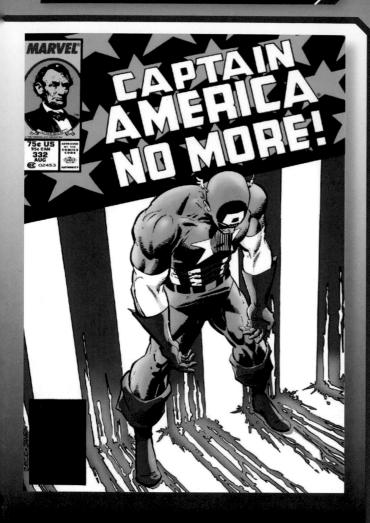

CAPTAIN AMERICA #332

"The way this room is set up is like something out of the Spanish Inquisition." CAPTAIN AMERICA

Main characters: Captain America; John Walker; Warhead
Supporting characters: General Wexler; Falcon; Demolition Man; Ms. Marvel (Carol Danvers); the Commission **Main locations:** Washington Monument; a hotel in Washington, DC; the Pentagon

BACKGROUND

As writer and editor, Mark Gruenwald chronicled Captain America's adventures for more than a decade. Beginning his career as an assistant editor in 1978, he worked at Marvel until his tragic death from a heart attack in 1996. His early *Captain America* issues remain some of the highlights of Cap's long history. Like many of the best comics, Mark's work reflected the real world at the time. By *Captain America* #332, he had already introduced John Walker, aka the Super-Patriot, an all-American hero who symbolized the lurch to the political right of the Reagan era. This made for some interesting comparisons with Steve Rogers' own views, established during President Roosevelt's New Deal era. During his time as writer, Gruenwald replaced Steve with John Walker (who later became U.S.Agent) and brought into play such memorable characters as Crossbones, Diamondback, and the Scourge of the Underworld.

The dilemma Steve faced this issue was powerfully depicted on the cover—Cap standing, head bowed, in front of a US flag dripping blood, with the Captain America icon replaced by Abraham Lincoln, another symbol of liberty and the American Dream. All of which set the scene for Steve quitting, with John Walker taking over as Cap the following issue. Steve would resume the role in *Captain America* #350, when the Red Skull was revealed to be the power behind the Commission on Superhuman Activities. This wasn't the first time Steve Rogers had given up the role of Captain America—and it wouldn't be the last.

August 1987

COVER ARTIST
Mike Zeck and Klaus Janson

EDITOR
Don Daley

WRITER
Mark Gruenwald

PENCILER
Tom Morgan

INKER
Bob McLeod

LETTERER
Diana Albers

COLORIST
Ken Feduniewicz

THE STORY

As a terrorist menaces Washington, DC, Steve Rogers faces his toughest decision—should he work for a secretive, right-wing government department, or stay true to his core beliefs and quit as Captain America?

1

2

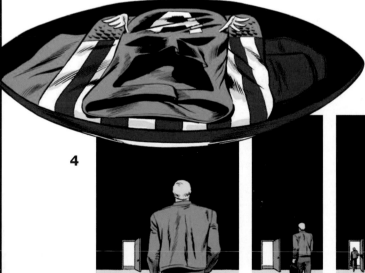

3

4

Crazy terrorist Warhead parachuted onto the Washington Monument, unfurling a sign that read, "Make war some more." It soon transpired he was armed not only with guns, but also with a thermonuclear device. Meanwhile, Steve Rogers arrived at the Pentagon to speak to General Wexler **(1)** about his recent run-in with G.I. Max, the government's latest version of a Super-Soldier. Cap was about to leave, his questions unanswered, when two FBI agents arrived and asked him to accompany them.

As the situation at the Washington Monument deteriorated, Cap found himself standing before the Commission on Superhuman Activities, a panel of politicians and security experts, which included the heads of the FBI and CIA. The Commission had transformed the Brotherhood of Mutants into a government superteam known as Freedom Force, and now had Cap in their sights, pointing out that when he agreed to become Captain America in 1941, he had signed up to serve as "America's official mascot." Captain America's uniform, shield, and even his name were all the property of the federal government. Cap explained that he'd been serving his country as part of the Avengers, but the Commission rejected his argument. Cap was now to report directly to the Commission, and if Steve refused, they would simply find another Captain America. Cap left with 24 hours to think it over **(2)**.

While Cap contemplated his future, the situation at the Monument grew more violent, with Warhead shooting at people below. John Walker, the Super-Patriot, and his friend Ethan, spotted a chance for the Super-Patriot to make his name. Cap, meanwhile, sought advice from his friends **(3)**, as he spent the night struggling with how to react to the Commission's demands. If he agreed to them, he would be forced to commit to missions that he might find morally objectionable.

Back at the monument, Warhead revealed that the bomb was created by S.H.I.E.L.D.'s adversary, A.I.M. He intended to unleash it if the US failed to declare war on another country—he believed that the nation was only truly great when at war with a common enemy. The Super-Patriot arrived and climbed the Monument, fighting with Warhead before hurling the villain from the top. As he fell to his death, Warhead pulled the pin on a hand grenade, choosing to go out "like a man"—in an explosion. The Super-Patriot returned to the ground with the nuke and handed it over to a cop, declaring that he'd done his part.

Meanwhile, Captain America had come to a decision. He returned to the Commission and delivered a powerful speech about how Captain America was no longer simply a soldier, but the kind of hero that truly embodied the American dream—a dream he believed would be corrupted if he worked for the Commission. Steve Rogers then handed back the shield and uniform **(4)**. He was no longer Captain America.

TASKMASTER

Tony Masters has the rare ability to study and perfectly replicate any displayed skill within minutes—something he refers to as photographic reflexes. Unfortunately, each time he commits a new skill to memory, it crowds out his regular memories, wiping memories of his past and leaving him an amnesiac.

ORIGINS

As an up-and-coming field agent for the counter-terrorism organization S.H.I.E.L.D., Tony Masters was determined to become the best at what he did. On one fateful mission, however, he was sent to capture former Nazi scientist Horst Gorscht, who had developed the flawed facsimile of the Super-Soldier serum that had powered villains from the World War II era like Master Man and Warrior Woman.

Gorscht and a team of SS soldiers had fled to South America after the war ended. The scientist had set up a laboratory in a castle in Bolivia where he set about cloning Hitler's brain and extracting the memories from it. He had also developed an injectable primer that gave a subject's brain the ability to absorb knowledge instantly. He planned to use this to implant Hitler's memories into every child born into his planned Fourth Reich.

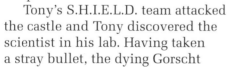

When Tony's team stormed Gorscht's castle, the doctor was shot by a stray bullet.

Tony's S.H.I.E.L.D. team attacked the castle and Tony discovered the scientist in his lab. Having taken a stray bullet, the dying Gorscht confessed all to Tony. Knowing that Gorscht would never have the chance to replicate his formula for his primer, Tony injected himself with it and fled.

The primer gave Tony the ability to learn any skill instantly, simply by exposing himself to it: fighting styles, languages, musical instruments, and so on. However, learning these skills took up a great deal of space in his brain and soon crowded out his regular memories, leaving him unaware of his past, including even his real name.

Tony took the moniker of Taskmaster and offered to train anyone who was willing to pay to learn a new skill. Tony's wife—a former S.H.I.E.L.D. agent named Mercedes Merced aka the Hub—directed him in his work. Despite her best efforts to help Tony remember things, she made no headway against his memory loss. Every time Tony used his powers, his memories of his wife would fade even further.

Taskmaster's original costume borrowed many elements from the Avengers, including Captain America's shield and boots.

"Anything the Avengers can do, I can do better!"

TASKMASTER

Taskmaster married Mercedes Merced when they both worked as S.H.I.E.L.D. agents. She now works with her amnesiac husband as his handler.

Taskmaster often found himself pitted against Captain America— a mercenary versus a man of high ideals.

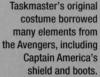

The skull mask is a tribute to Santa Muerte, a Mexican figure called Saint Death, Lady of Shadows.

TRAINING DAYS

In addition to his work as a mercenary, Tony sold his services as a military trainer. As well as instructing the minions for countless criminal networks—including A.I.M. and Hydra—and Super Villains Crossbones and the Red Skull, Tony has also trained those associated with anti-terrorism, such as John Walker (the man who temporarily replaced Steve Rogers as Cap). He even became the drill sergeant at Camp Hammond where he worked for the Avengers Academy.

Taskmaster's shield helps him copy Cap's moves. However, it is not indestructible as it is made using an osmium, rather than Vibranium, alloy.

DATA FILE

FIRST APPEARANCE: *Avengers* #195 (April 1980)

REAL NAME: Tony Masters

AFFILIATIONS: A.I.M., Avengers, Deadpool, Finesse, Hydra, the Org, S.H.I.E.L.D., Thunderbolts.

POWERS AND ABILITIES: Tony's photographic reflexes can duplicate any physical action or skill by simply studying it for a minute or two. If he watches the action in double time, he can perform it at double speed. Having closely studied many superhumans, Tony is a world-class athlete and acrobat as well as an expert in all kinds of combat and weaponry.

Taskmaster brandishes a sword identical to that of the former Avengers member Black Knight, and copies the moves of the Super Villain Swordsman.

SIN

As the daughter of the Red Skull, Sinthea Shmidt always strove to live up to her father's levels of hatred and evil. She had a brief childhood, since her father accelerated her age using his "Deus Machina." Calling herself Sin, she joined in her father's plans to kill Captain America, and she eventually took on the Red Skull title.

As Mother Superior, Sin ruled over the Sisters of Sin and aided her father in his plans to kill Captain America and his friends in the Avengers.

ORIGINS

Eager to create a legacy for himself as he aged, the Red Skull decided to produce an heir. He fathered a child with a washerwoman who died in childbirth. When he found out that he had a daughter rather than a son, the Red Skull was so angry that he set out immediately to kill the baby girl. One of his followers—who later became Mother Night—pointed out that his blood ran in his daughter's veins. The Red Skull changed his mind and charged the woman with training the girl, named Sinthea, to become the hateful person she would need to be to inherit all he had labored over. Despite this plan, he doubted she could ever fill his boots.

Eager for Sinthea to grow up, the Red Skull used a machine to artificially age his young daughter into a fully grown woman. The process also endowed her with superpowers. In addition, the Red Skull put four young orphan girls through the same aging process and called them the Sisters of Sin. He put his daughter Sinthea in charge of them, giving her the title Mother Superior. Later, Mother Night took over the group, and Sinthea went by the name of Sin.

The Red Skull used his "Deus Machina" to fill Sinthea's mind with evil thoughts.

The security agency S.H.I.E.L.D. captured Sin and reprogrammed her to be a regular young woman, but the Super Villain Crossbones—who was working for the Red Skull—kidnapped Sin and tortured her until her original personality emerged. The pair then entered into a relationship. They united with the Red Skull—whose mind was in the body of former Russian general Aleksander Lukin—in a plan to kill Captain America and then transfer the Red Skull's mind into Cap's body. When that plan failed, the Red Skull's mind was forced into a robotic body that exploded, killing what was left of the villain. Sin was caught in the blast, and the damage from it caused the skin on her head to turn red and all her hair to fall out. Sin embraced her new look and without her father around to object, she took up his legacy, claiming herself to be the new Red Skull.

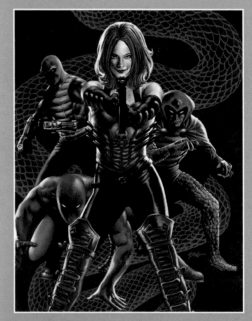

Sin formed a new version of the mercenary group the Serpent Squad to once again help execute her father's plans.

"Farewell, Skull. No one will miss you." SIN

Sin and Crossbones began a relationship when Crossbones kidnapped her from S.H.I.E.L.D. custody. He worked with her when she became the new Red Skull.

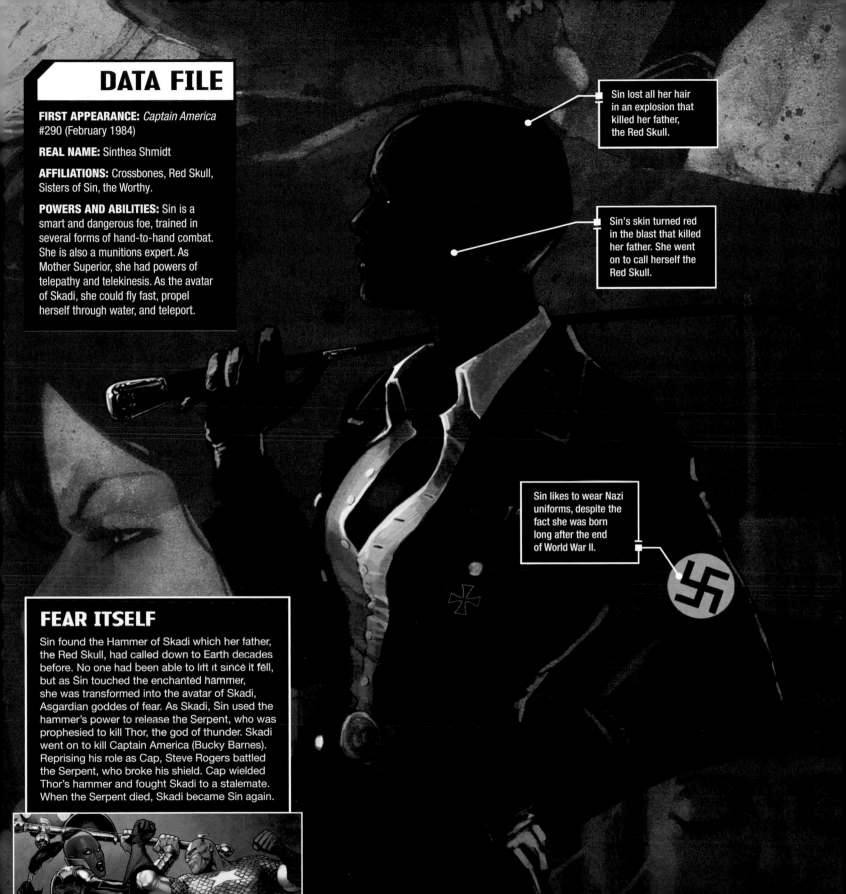

DATA FILE

FIRST APPEARANCE: *Captain America* #290 (February 1984)

REAL NAME: Sinthea Shmidt

AFFILIATIONS: Crossbones, Red Skull, Sisters of Sin, the Worthy.

POWERS AND ABILITIES: Sin is a smart and dangerous foe, trained in several forms of hand-to-hand combat. She is also a munitions expert. As Mother Superior, she had powers of telepathy and telekinesis. As the avatar of Skadi, she could fly fast, propel herself through water, and teleport.

Sin lost all her hair in an explosion that killed her father, the Red Skull.

Sin's skin turned red in the blast that killed her father. She went on to call herself the Red Skull.

Sin likes to wear Nazi uniforms, despite the fact she was born long after the end of World War II.

FEAR ITSELF

Sin found the Hammer of Skadi which her father, the Red Skull, had called down to Earth decades before. No one had been able to lift it since it fell, but as Sin touched the enchanted hammer, she was transformed into the avatar of Skadi, Asgardian goddes of fear. As Skadi, Sin used the hammer's power to release the Serpent, who was prophesied to kill Thor, the god of thunder. Skadi went on to kill Captain America (Bucky Barnes). Reprising his role as Cap, Steve Rogers battled the Serpent, who broke his shield. Cap wielded Thor's hammer and fought Skadi to a stalemate. When the Serpent died, Skadi became Sin again.

CROSSBONES

A mercenary who trained with Taskmaster, Brock worked with the Red Skull and fell in love with the villain's daughter, Sinthea Shmidt, aka Sin. As the Super Villain Crossbones, Brock is best known for assassinating Captain America on the steps of a federal courthouse in New York after the close of the Superhuman Civil War.

Crossbones took great pleasure in abusing Diamondback several times over the years, but she eventually got her revenge.

ORIGINS

Brock Rumlow grew up poor on the Lower East Side of Manhattan, where he fell in with a gang of white supremacists known as the Savage Crims. After he raped 15-year-old Rachel Leighton (later known as Diamondback), two of Rachel's brothers came after him for revenge. He killed them both and fled. Brock entered a school run by Taskmaster—a villain with photographic reflexes—and became one of his top students. After graduation, he was hired to help train others, and went on to become a mercenary. For a while he worked for the 1950s Red Skull, Albert Malik, under the codename Frag. Under Albert's orders, he attacked Arnim Zola's home in Switzerland in a disastrous operation of which he was the sole survivor. He impressed the original Red Skull enough, though, that he was taken under his wing and given the name Crossbones. Brock has been loyal to the Red Skull ever since.

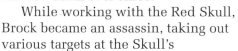

Cap saves Diamondback from Crossbones and his evil Skeleton Crew.

> "I consider myself an artist—a true craftsman who specializes in murder, destruction, and terror." CROSSBONES

Crossbones fell in love with Sin while working for her father, the Red Skull. He rescued her from S.H.I.E.L.D. custody and brought her back to serve the Red Skull with him.

While working with the Red Skull, Brock became an assassin, taking out various targets at the Skull's instruction. He even led the first version of the Red Skull's Skeleton Crew, which included Mother Night, Machinesmith, the fourth Sleeper robot, and the Voice. When he dared to question the Red Skull's decision to recruit Viper, though, he was fired. Crossbones immediately left the team, happy not to have been killed, as so often happened with the Red Skull's minions.

To get back into the Red Skull's good graces, Brock tracked down and kidnapped his former victim, Rachel, who was dating Captain America at the time. He tried to brainwash her into betraying Cap, but she double-crossed him. When Brock returned to the Red Skull's employ, he had been replaced as the leader of the Skeleton Crew by Cutthroat—who was Rachel's third brother, Danny Leighton. Cutthroat tried to murder Brock in his sleep, but Brock slew him instead.

Crossbones appreciated the Red Skull's hateful vision for conquering the world, and he worked alongside Sin and Red Skull as often as he could.

Crossbones wears a cowl with a white skull design on it to intimidate his opponents, as well as to conceal his identity.

While Crossbones is deadly in combat, he prefers to use automatic weapons when he wants to kill lots of people at once.

The crossed bone pattern featured on the breastplate is part of the pirate symbol. It declares that Crossbones follows no law but his own.

DATA FILE

FIRST APPEARANCE: *Captain America* #359 (October 1989)

REAL NAME: Brock Rumlow

AFFILIATIONS: A.I.M., Baron Helmut Zemo, Hydra, the Red Skull, Sin, Skeleton Crew, Thunderbolts

POWERS AND ABILITIES: Brock is an expert in several martial arts and is gifted with weapons and firearms. He also has some experience with brainwashing others.

KILLING CAPTAIN AMERICA—AND BEYOND

Brock played a huge role in Cap's assassination after the Superhuman Civil War. Using a sniper rifle, he fired the bullet that brought down Cap on the steps of the federal courthouse in New York City—but didn't actually kill him. The Falcon and Bucky (as the Winter Soldier) captured Brock and turned him over to anti-terrorism agency, S.H.I.E.L.D. Later, after Cap returned, Brock worked for Luke Cage's version of the Thunderbolts, a team comprised of supposedly reformed criminals. He was exposed to vapor from the Terrigen Mists which enabled him to fire energy beams, but this power did not last.

DEATH OF THE RED SKULL

The scene was set for a final showdown between two archenemies: the Red Skull and Captain America. Could this signal the end of an era for the two foes?

NO ONE IS SAFE

Life was good for Captain America, who had assembled a rich roster of supportive characters. He had a love interest in Bernie Rosenthal, close friends in Arnie Roth and Dave Cox, a crime-fighting partner in Falcon, and a whole Super Hero team of Avengers ready to come to his aid. But the Red Skull—and his associate Baron Zemo and daughter Sin—struck at the heart of Cap's personal network. The Red Skull organized the kidnapping of Bernie, Arnie, and the Falcon. His goal was to goad Cap into a final showdown, one in which he thought both men would perish and continue their struggle in the afterlife. Cap had to put everything on the line to stop this mad scheme and save his friends from psychological torture inside the dark depths of his archenemy's Gothic mansion, Skull House.

Cap and the Red Skull, physically weakened to match their chronological ages, fight with the desperation of dying men.

THE FIRST VICTIM

Sin, the Red Skull's daughter, was also Mother Superior—leader of the Super Villain group the Sisters of Sin. She hoped to bring another villain onto her side. This was Baron Helmut Zemo, who had always blamed Captain America for the death of his father. Sin, Zemo, and the Red Skull joined forces to take revenge on their hated enemy. Their first target was Dave Cox, a one-armed military veteran and peace activist who was also a close ally of Cap. Sin captured him and subjected him to brainwashing, turning Dave Cox into the costumed killer the Slayer.

While he was transformed into the Slayer, Dave Cox wore the cape and costume of Super Villain Devil-Slayer. He brandished a mace.

> "We will pass the boundaries of life with our souls entwined, and grapple for all eternity!"

THE RED SKULL

INSIDE SKULL HOUSE

Captain America defeated his crazed colleague, but more unpleasant surprises were quick to follow. Arnie Roth, another old friend, became a prisoner of Baron Zemo and Sin. Tracking Arnie to Skull House, Cap and his partner Nomad were attacked by the Sisters of Sin. Meanwhile, the Falcon, and Cap's love Bernie Rosenthal became the newest prisoners in Skull House's dungeon. It was up to Captain America to save them all, but he had been given a poison that was slowly aging his body to that of an elderly man.

THE CONFRONTATION

Eventually Captain America was maneuvered into a subterranean bunker beneath Skull House, where the Red Skull was waiting. When Cap's foe pulled his mask loose, his physical appearance matched the aged condition of his body. The Red Skull was dying, and his master plan was for the two of them to perish together in a final, fatal battle.

RED SKULL'S FATE

The two aged men fought it out in a final showdown. Cap eventually bested the Red Skull, who then succumbed to a heart attack and passed away in the arms of his enemy. After making a full recovery, Cap left Skull House carrying his foe's lifeless body. It was time to bury the past and look ahead to the future.

137

CAP RETURNS

Captain America (John Walker) was pitted against the Captain (Steve Rogers). Was this something to do with the newly resurrected Red Skull?

Following John Walker's defeat by the Flag-Smasher, the political powers that be were not convinced that he was up to the job of Captain America. With his role as Cap in question, Walker was lured into a trap set by the newly resurrected Red Skull where he was pitted against various costumed foes. The Red Skull had been secretly manipulating members of the government to do his bidding and was now occupying the cloned body of a Super-Soldier. With his new muscle-bound appearance, the Red Skull was ready to defeat Cap and gain more political power.

Meanwhile, the Captain (Steve Rogers) was hot on the trail of Cap, planning to return his shield, which he had acquired while fighting the Flag-Smasher. He tracked Cap to a building where he ended up battling a raging Walker. When Steve defeated Walker, the Red Skull appeared in his new disguise. However, when Walker exposed him to the Dust of Death, Skull was left with scars that gave him a "red skull" appearance. Before he could be apprehended, the Red Skull escaped. Walker returned Cap's uniform to Steve.

POLITICAL MANEUVERING

The US government's Commission on Superhuman Affairs met to discuss John Walker's performance as Captain America. His recklessness and his refusal to obey orders were too much for the Commission, which voted to suspend Walker from the role pending an official investigation. President Ronald Reagan made a surprise visit and began asking questions about who should be in the Captain America role. The members of the Commission, under fire from their boss, wondered what to do next.

FLAG-SMASHER

A crisis erupted in an Arctic research station where the anti-nationalist Flag-Smasher was holding hostages and insisting that he speak with Captain America. The Commission sent John Walker to handle the situation, but the less experienced hero was overcome and kidnapped by Flag-Smasher.

THE CAPTAIN INTERVENES

The Flag-Smasher sent a message demanding to speak with the real Captain America. Steve Rogers answered the call. In his guise of the Captain, he rescued Walker, learning from Flag-Smasher that the Red Skull might have returned.

"I am Captain America. There is only one!"

JOHN WALKER AS
CAPTAIN AMERICA

THE NEW RED SKULL

Steve Rogers' worst fears were confirmed in Washington, DC, where the Red Skull had become a political power broker, and had been pulling the strings of the Commission all along. The Red Skull now inhabited a Super-Soldier body cloned from Steve's own, and was his enemy's physical equal.

SALUTE TO STEVE ROGERS

Following Walker's defeat at the hands of Steve Rogers, the Red Skull spoke to Steve, but accidentally inhaled a cloud of poisonous dust. The toxin transformed his face into a permanent, skull-like horror and he fled. In the aftermath, a humbled Walker handed over the uniform and the iconic shield of Captain America to Steve. Cap was back—the original and the best!

In an effort to recover the shield he had lost in the Arctic, John Walker was lured into a trap where he was forced to fight costumed combatants at the behest of the Red Skull. Steve Rogers arrived to deliver Cap's shield back to him, but the unhinged John Walker was goaded by the Red Skull into fighting Steve. The veteran finally triumphed over his younger rival.

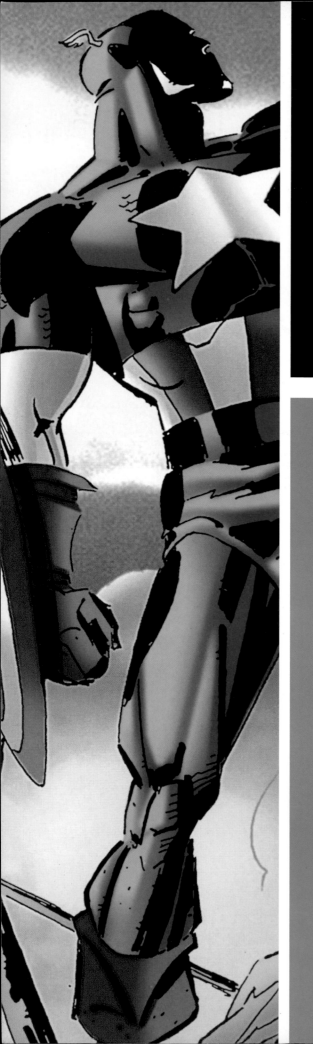

THE
19

The 1990s were an unsettling time for Cap, as Marvel reinvented him a number of times, trying to connect him with modern audiences.

At a time of relative peace, Captain America once again struggled to find a purpose. Writer and editor Mark Gruenwald ended a ten-year run on *Captain America* in 1995, with Cap's apparent death caused by the Super-Soldier serum. The title passed to Mark Waid, who with artist Ron Garney would be responsible for some of Cap's greatest storylines.

Less than a year later, the series was canceled and rebooted with a new #1 issue—the first since 1940—which introduced a different version of Cap, awakening in an altered universe. This was part of the "Onslaught" event, in which several heroes were thought to have sacrificed themselves to stop the villain Onslaught. In fact, Franklin Richards (son of Mr. Fantastic and the Invisible Woman) had transported them to a pocket universe. *Captain America* was one of a few titles given to creators known for their work with Image Comics, with Jeph Loeb and Rob Liefeld taking on Cap's story.

In January 1998, Cap and the other heroes returned to the regular Marvel Universe, and the previous team of Waid and Garney began their second run with another brand-new *Captain America* #1.

OVERLEAF

Captain America Vol. 3 #12 (December 1998): When he was captured, along with Sharon, in the demon Nightmare's dimension, Cap prevented a full-on nuclear catastrophe by drawing on the power of the American dream.
Cover art: Andy Kubert

90s

TIME AND SPACE

Cap's varied adventures have taken him through space and time, briefly turning him into a werewolf and bringing him close to death.

HAPPY ANNIVERSARY

Father Time (an Elder of the Universe) sent Cap on a tour through America's past where he met other icons like conservationist Johnny Appleseed, cowboy Pecos Bill, steel-driver John Henry, giant lumberjack Paul Bunyan, and 19th-century symbol of America Uncle Sam. Cap's travels were an elaborate illusion, and a ploy to keep him busy so the Avengers could arrange an anniversary party for him.

The party was meant to celebrate the 50th anniversary of Steve Rogers becoming Cap, but Father Time had other ideas for how Cap should spend the day.

The historical American legends, like Johnny Appleseed, stood ready to lend a hand to Captain America—even if they thought he dressed funny.

Thanos—an Eternal from Titan—fell in love with the cosmic entity Death. In a bid to impress her, Thanos sought incredible power using the Infinity Gauntlet. He became so powerful he wiped out half the lives in the universe as an offering to her. These lives were later restored.

INFINITY WARS

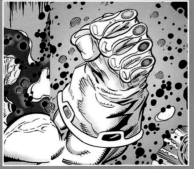

Cap helped Earth's heroes defeat the mad Titan, named Thanos. He had taken control of the universe using an artifact that contained six gems of incredible power, known as the Infinity Gauntlet. An artificially created human called Adam Warlock took custody of the gauntlet, but this freed his future evil self—the Magus—to start a new war, pitting evil versions of the heroes against themselves.

Each gem in the Infinity Gauntlet controls a particular domain: mind (blue), power (red), reality (yellow), soul (green), space (purple), and time (orange).

CAP BY NIGHT

While looking for his former pilot John Jameson—aka Man-Wolf—Captain America was turned into a werewolf by a serum developed by the villain Nightshade, who was one of the Femizons working for criminal scientist Superia. Nightshade lost control of him, though, because the werewolf serum conflicted with his Super-Soldier serum. Nightshade was coerced into developing a cure for Cap's werewolf problem.

THE IRON CAP

The Super-Soldier serum that gave Cap his powers was deteriorating and would soon kill him. He donned a suit of powered armor to help sustain him through his last 24 hours. Cap appeared to die, but he was later revived with help from S.H.I.E.L.D. operative Sharon Carter and a blood transfusion from the Red Skull.

CAP'S FORCE SHIELD

Soon after his return from the Heroes Reborn world, Captain America lost his shield in the ocean. For a while, he used a replica of his triangular shield, but after it was damaged, S.H.I.E.L.D. agent Sharon Carter brought him an electronic version, created by a force-field projector built into his glove. It simulated Vibranium, allowing it to absorb and return energy.

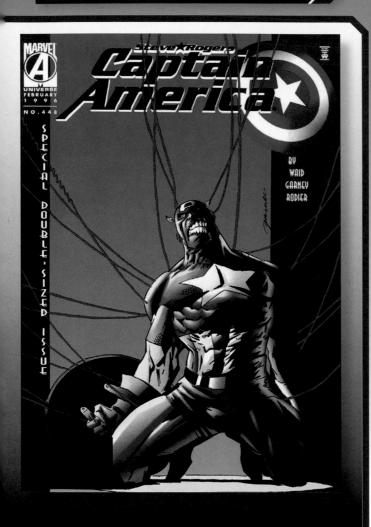

MARVEL
UNIVERSE
FEBRUARY
1996
NO. 448

Steve Rogers
Captain America

SPECIAL DOUBLE-SIZED ISSUE

BY
WAID
GARNEY
RODIER

February 1996

COVER ARTIST, PENCILER
Ron Garney

EDITOR
Ralph Macchio

WRITER
Mark Waid

INKER
Denis Rodier

LETTERER
John Costanza

COLORIST
John Kalisz

CAPTAIN AMERICA #448

"*Tell me something, Skull… tell me there's a way I won't kill you!*" CAPTAIN AMERICA

Main characters: Captain America; the Red Skull; Sharon Carter **Supporting characters:** Bucky Barnes; Nick Fury; Human Torch; Sub-Mariner; Dr. Erskine; Baron Zemo **Main locations:** Manhattan; inside the Cosmic Cube

BACKGROUND *Captain America* #448 was the double-issue finale to "Operation Rebirth," writer Mark Waid and artist Ron Garney's first story arc. The pair had started to chronicle Steve Rogers' adventures in *Captain America* #444, which dealt with the ramifications of Cap's apparent death, once the Super-Soldier serum finally failed. In an increasingly cynical world, the adventures of the patriotic Captain America had begun to feel anachronistic, but under Waid and Garney his role was revitalized, their storylines reflecting the real-world politics of the time.

It turned out that Cap had survived his death, thanks to his archenemy the Red Skull and his former girlfriend Sharon Carter (who he believed had been killed in action years before). Sharon was working with the Red Skull to save Steve Rogers and stop an even greater threat—Adolf Hitler. Hitler's consciousness had survived World War II thanks to Arnim Zola, who had transferred it to a clone of Hitler known as the Hate-Monger. Now this consciousness was contained in a Cosmic Cube, a reality-altering object that the Skull had stolen from A.I.M.. From within the Cube, Hitler was recreating an alternate reality in which the Reich ruled the world. Cap had managed to get hold of the Cube, but he had been tricked by the Red Skull and became trapped inside it.

This critically acclaimed run of Captain America was cut short, but Marvel listened to its readership, and after a year of "Heroes Reborn," Waid and Garney returned to Captain America with a brand-new story arc, starting in January 1998.

THE STORY

Unknowingly trapped in a Cosmic Cube by the Red Skull, Captain America targets Hitler's bunker in the last days of World War II. But if he succeeds in defeating the Führer, he will be giving victory to the Red Skull…

Inside the Cosmic Cube, Steve Rogers was reliving the time that he became Captain America. As soon as Dr. Erskine had administered the Super-Soldier serum, a German assassin tried to kill him—but Steve leaped into the line of fire and saved the doctor. Immediately, Bucky Barnes appeared, urging Steve to join him and fight the Nazis. In the real world, the Red Skull gloated. He held in his hand the Cosmic Cube, watching as Cap met Bucky inside **(1)**. Also trapped in the Cube was Hitler's consciousness, which had to be destroyed if the Red Skull was to harness the Cube's power for himself. The Skull believed only one person was capable of killing Hitler, and that was why he had saved Cap's life—and why he now had him trapped in the Cube. Cap would create his own reality inside the Cube, one where he killed the Führer, and at that moment the Cosmic Cube's power would belong to the Skull.

Cap found himself back in wartime New York City with Bucky, fighting German agents who had taken over a radio station inside the Empire State Building. As they chased a Nazi spy onto the roof, Cap found himself suddenly on one of the Twin Towers. Confused, Cap followed Bucky up a ladder attached to a futuristic airship. On board, the villainous Baron Zemo had captured Bucky and tied him to a drone. Cap then relived the moment when Bucky had died—but this time he saved him and gained control of the drone, returning to the airship. They used it to travel to Berlin, and arrived just as Nick Fury and the Howling Commandos were cutting a path toward Hitler's bunker, helped by the Human Torch and Sub-Mariner **(2)**.

As Cap and Bucky approached Hitler's bunker, Bucky stopped—something wasn't right. Cap's consciousness had been telling him this wasn't real, through hints at first, but now

Bucky was openly saying that this wasn't Cap's world. He told Cap that the mission to kill Hitler was a trap. Cap approached the door to the bunker and burst through into the real world, where a shocked Red Skull was unable to comprehend how Cap had the willpower to escape the Cube. The pair fought **(3)**, and as the Skull made a desperate attempt to reach the fallen Cube, Cap hurled his shield at the villain—cutting the Skull's arm off and shattering the Cube. The ensuing explosion claimed both the Skull and the Cube, leaving nothing of Cap's enemy but an ashen shadow on the wall. Reality reasserted itself around them, soldiers who had been transformed into Reich members returning to normal. Cap then came face-to-face with Sharon **(4)**, who he believed had been killed in action years before, and set out to discover why S.H.I.E.L.D. had lied to him.

SUPERIA

The brilliant and power-mad scientist Dr. Deidre Wentworth transformed herself into Superia. As the founder of the private island of Femizonia, the Super Villain set about trying to create an alternate future in which 95% of the world's women had been made infertile and the men had been enslaved.

When Superia wants something, like the command of the criminal organization A.I.M., she takes it. She does not hesitate to use lethal force.

ORIGINS

Dr. Deidre Wentworth became Superia to prove the superiority of women—by turning the men of the world into her slaves. She hated men and strove to create a future in which they would become unnecessary. She claimed to be the ancestor of Thundra, a superhuman woman from a possible future in which nearly all women had been rendered infertile in a horrible disaster that had led the women of that world to enslave the men. Superia learned this by means of a time probe that brought her the information from the future.

To guarantee that Thundra's future would happen, Deidre set about creating the disaster herself. She gathered over ten thousand women—including many superhumans—on an island she dubbed "Femizonia," home to her "Femizons." Superia enlisted Diamondback in her cause, unaware that the snake-costumed Super Hero was Captain America's girlfriend. When Cap and the private investigator Paladin came searching for Diamondback, Superia and her army captured the two men, and Superia took them to her lab to chemically transform them into women. With the help of her friends, Diamondback freed Cap and Paladin, and then helped them thwart Deidre's plans.

Soon after, Deidre joined global terrorist group A.I.M. When Cap was dying from a flaw in the Super-Soldier serum, she devised a cure and tried to use it to blackmail him. When Cap refused, the Red Skull—who was in a body cloned from Cap's and was suffering from the same troubles—took the cure for himself. He then killed Superia to keep her from helping Cap.

Superia later returned from the dead and tried to take over what was now the criminal organization, H.A.M.M.E.R. However, the Super Hero group the New Avengers stopped her cold. Soon after, she became a part of criminal mastermind Norman Osborn's new Dark Avengers, taking the position of Ms. Marvel, but when that effort folded, she returned to A.I.M.

A stylized version of the astrological symbol for Venus appears on Superia's outfit.

"Greetings, my sisters, and welcome to Femizonia!" SUPERIA

In an alternate timeline, Superia sent her mind back in time to a younger version of herself. She then became the patriotic "hero" Broad-Stripe and joined the Avengers.

When Norman Osborn formed his new team of Dark Avengers—a group of villains posing as heroes—Superia took on the title of Ms. Marvel.

FIRST APPEARANCE: *Captain America* #390 (August 1991)

REAL NAME: Deidre Wentworth

AFFILIATIONS: A.I.M., Femizons, H.A.M.M.E.R., Thundra

POWERS AND ABILITIES: Deidre has superhuman strength and durability, and she can fly and fire energy blasts from her hands. She is a scientific genius and a master of many forms of martial arts.

Superia does not always wear a costume to work. She's smart enough to try to avoid attention when she can.

Superia stands six-and-a-half feet tall. She creates a formidable presence.

Superia has the ability to fire energy blasts from her hands.

THE SUPERIA REALITY

The moment she was supposedly killed by the Red Skull, Deidre thrust her mind back to a much younger self. The younger Deidre worked to create a new reality, one in which Captain America never returned after World War II and in which she controlled much of America. She set herself up as a new patriotic hero named Broad-Stripe, partnered with a woman she transformed into Bright Star. To stop her, the immortal being known as Contemplator brought together five different Caps from across time: Steve Rogers, John Walker, Bucky, American Dream (a future cousin of Sharon Carter), and Commander A (from the 25th century).

OPERATION: REBIRTH

In an unlikely alliance, Cap and the Red Skull fought against a common enemy. But it wasn't long before the Skull showed his true colors.

An alliance between Captain America and his greatest foe, the Red Skull, seemed impossible. But the two teamed up to stop a common enemy—Hitler, the Red Skull's former mentor—who was trying to use the powers of the Cosmic Cube to take control of the world.

Cap had been missing in action, and was presumed dead, but his friend and S.H.I.E.L.D. agent Sharon Carter helped bring him back from the dead in a secret laboratory, allowing the Super-Soldier and the Red Skull to embark on a covert mission to put an end to Hitler's plan.

As the mission unfolded, however, the Red Skull revealed his true intentions: to trap Cap together with Hitler in the Cosmic Cube so that he could have absolute power over the world. Even though Cap's body was not in peak Super-Soldier physical condition, he was able to defend himself against the Red Skull, and ultimately save the world from his evil intentions.

AN IMPOSSIBLE ALLIANCE

Cap was missing in action, presumed dead. But in a secret laboratory, S.H.I.E.L.D. agent Sharon Carter oversaw the hero's resurrection, thanks to a blood transfusion from the Red Skull. Cap's nemesis had his own reasons for helping rejuvenate the former American Super-Soldier, but he wasn't about to reveal them just yet!

SURPRISE MISSION

Following his rebirth, Cap, Sharon, and the Red Skull raided the A.I.M (Advanced Idea Mechanics) secure facility that stored the Cosmic Cube. As he fought the guards, Cap felt his strength returning, and realized that his blood transfusion had come from a Super-Soldier. He discovered that his donor had been the Red Skull, whose cloned body was a duplicate of his own.

THE CUBE'S SECRET

Cap learned the reason behind the strange team-up. Inside the Cosmic Cube was the consciousness of the former Hate-Monger Adolf Hitler, who would gain absolute power once he took control of the Cube. The group battled its way toward the artifact, but Hitler's mind transformed the A.I.M. agents into armed soldiers of the New World Reich.

TRAPPED IN THE CUBE

As Cap dealt with the threat, the Red Skull revealed the true reason why he wanted his nemesis on this mission. His plan was to trap Cap inside the Cosmic Cube where he would face Hitler. With his two archenemies battling it out, the Red Skull would be able to use the Cube's powers unchallenged. Inside the Cube, Cap had an illusion where he saw Bucky and overcame some of his past tragedies.

STOPPING THE SKULL

Captain America ultimately chose reality over fantasy. He broke out of the Cube and attacked the Red Skull. The damaged Cosmic Cube exploded, vaporizing into nonexistence and taking the Red Skull with it.

HEROES REBORN

Following a battle with the powerful villain Onslaught, Cap was thrown into an alternate reality with a completely new history.

A fight with the psionic entity known as Onslaught flung Cap into a parallel universe without any memory of his former life. Steve Rogers went about his daily life in the American suburbs with a perfect wife and son, but his true identity did not stay hidden for very long.

Steve was still Captain America, but his memory had been tampered with. Cap was informed that his civilian life was a cover-up, which was set up to protect his identity until he was needed by the anti-terrorist agency known as S.H.I.E.L.D. Steve subsequently learned that this was not the first time he had been controlled and "deactivated" by the government.

Finally, Steve realized that he had to take on the identity of Captain America once more in order to defeat the two deadly villains the Red Skull and Master Man. His return to the Super Hero world led to a massive battle that shook the globe. Ultimately, the parallel universe came to an end and Cap was able to return to the real world.

THE TRUTH

Steve Rogers appeared to be the perfect American father, with a loving wife and son. But unbeknownst to him, his memory had been wiped and he was in fact a government Super-Soldier. He was soon forced to confront his past, however, when an old man named Abraham Wilson told Rogers that he was really Captain America and presented him with a shield as proof.

SECRET SUPER-SOLDIER

Steve got the full story from Nick Fury, the director of S.H.I.E.L.D. He told Steve that his wife and son were really android duplicates and that his suburban life was a deep-cover illusion to keep him occupied until he was called back to duty. Steve learned that he had been honored for his heroism as far back as World War II.

HISTORY OF SERVICE

During the Korean War, Steve had been reactivated as Captain John Battle and subsequently in the Vietnam War, he was Captain Jack Strike. When Steve learned of the threat posed by the Red Skull and Master Man, he was willing to reclaim his heroic persona, as long as he would be the one calling the shots.

ATTACK ON AMERICA

Cap's return could not have come at a better time. The Red Skull and Master Man were planning a takeover of the US, backed by the racial-purity recruits of the extremist group the World Party, and an arsenal of nuclear warheads. Dance-enthusiast Rebecca "Rikki" Barnes infiltrated the World Party to rescue her brother, who was a recruit, and found herself fighting on the same side as Cap and his new ally Sam Wilson, son of Abraham. They stopped the countdown for the launch of the World Party's nukes—saving America.

UNIVERSE'S END

Moving out from under the control of spy agency S.H.I.E.L.D., Captain America teamed up with Rikki Barnes on voyages across the nation and fought the evil forces of Dr. Doom. Ultimately, a climactic battle shook the world, ending this mirror version of Steve Rogers and allowing Cap to return to his normal reality.

CAPTAIN AMERICA #402
JULY 1992

In the search for his missing colleagues John Jameson (aka Man-Wolf) and Diamondback, Cap embarked on a six-part story "Man and Wolf" that saw him turned into a werewolf known as Capwolf. Cover art: Rik Levins and Danny Bulanadi

THE
20

With the advent of the War on Terror, America needed its most patriotic hero to step up one more time.

The relative peace of the 1990s shattered on September 11, 2001, when al-Qaeda terrorists hijacked commercial jets and crashed the planes into the World Trade Center and the Pentagon. Captain America once again answered the call to defend America with a relaunch of his title under the purview of writer John Ney Rieber and artist John Cassaday. The first issue opened with Steve Rogers helping to dig through the rubble at Ground Zero, where the World Trade Center once stood in New York City.

Soon enough, Cap's old enemies demanded his attention again, and writer Ed Brubaker stepped in to chronicle Cap's new adventures in a darker, more modern era. His run lasted eight years and thrust Cap into a web of intrigue and twisted histories. This saw the return of Bucky as the Winter Soldier and the death of Captain America by means of a plot of the Red Skull. Later in the decade, Cap's sidekick Bucky took up the shield and became the new Captain America.

Steve Rogers eventually resumed his role as Captain America, but he aged rapidly in more recent years and gave up the shield once more. This time, Steve Rogers personally handed over his shield and title to one of his greatest friends: Sam Wilson, aka the Falcon.

OVERLEAF

Steve Rogers: Super-Soldier #1 (September 2010): After Steve Rogers returned from the dead, he let Bucky carry on in his role as Captain America while Rogers was dedicated to working behind the scenes.
Cover art: Carlos Pacheco, Tim Townsend, and Frank D'Armata

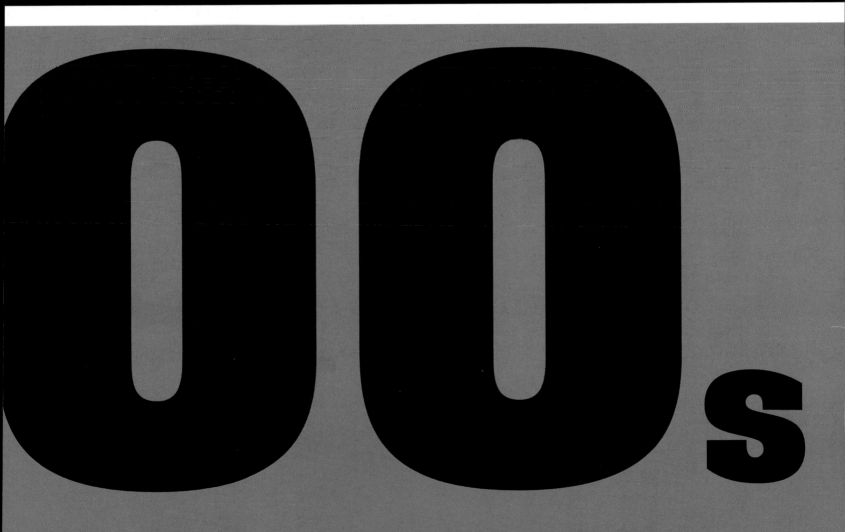

OOs

SERIES OF UNFORTUNATE EVENTS

Cap has had to face some of his biggest, most complex challenges since the start of the new millennium.

AVENGERS DISASSEMBLED

Once the Scarlet Witch discovered that her memories of her children with the android the Vision had been erased—because they had never truly existed—she went insane. She set about destroying the Avengers from within and by the time she was finished, Cap was truly without a team of Super Heroes.

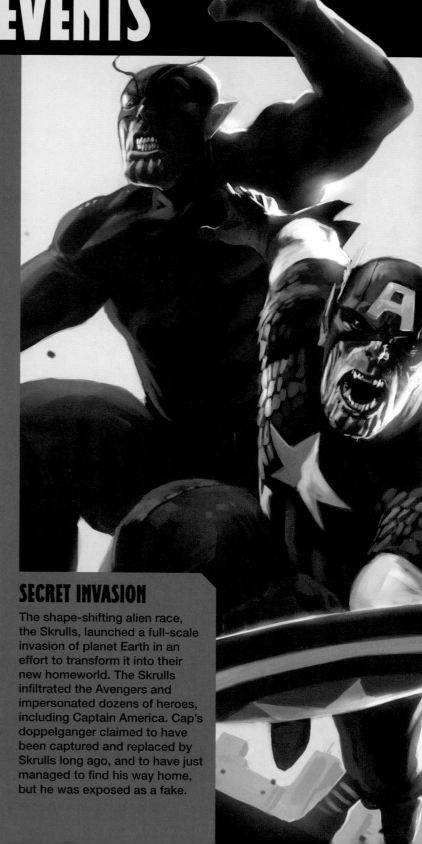

SECRET INVASION

The shape-shifting alien race, the Skrulls, launched a full-scale invasion of planet Earth in an effort to transform it into their new homeworld. The Skrulls infiltrated the Avengers and impersonated dozens of heroes, including Captain America. Cap's doppelganger claimed to have been captured and replaced by Skrulls long ago, and to have just managed to find his way home, but he was exposed as a fake.

INFINITY

When the ultrapowerful aliens known as the Builders decided to attack Earth, Captain America led a team of the world's most powerful Avengers to meet the invading force in space, before it could actually reach Earth. Working with the Galactic Council, the Avengers also helped to free other planets under the Builders' control, forming an alliance that could hope to face up to the enemy.

TIME RUNS OUT

In an interdimensional disaster known as an incursion, the multiverse started to collapse, causing alternate Earths to collide with each other. When the intellectual think tank, the Illuminati, began preparing to destroy planets that threatened Earth, Cap stood against the group—and was kicked out with his memory of the Illuminati wiped. In the end, only the Ultimate Earth and Marvel Earth remained, but were soon replaced by Battleworld.

HOUSE OF M

Her insanity growing, the Scarlet Witch transformed Earth into one in which mutants, led by her father Magneto, ruled. In this reality, Cap never disappeared at the end of World War II. Instead, he had married French Resistance fighter Peggy Carter, had become an astronaut, and was the first man on the moon! In this alternate world, Cap became marginalized for speaking out against Magneto's regime.

THE ANTI-CAP

After his girlfriend perished in the Oklahoma City bombing, the man who would become the Anti-Cap tried to enlist in the Navy, but was turned down. Later, he became the subject of a military experiment that transformed him into a Super-Soldier. But not everything went to plan, and Cap had to deal with an Anti-Cap who had gone rogue.

The morning of the bombing of the Federal Building in Oklahoma City, the Anti-Cap's girlfriend had agreed to go steady with him. They never got the chance to celebrate.

ORIGINS

The Anti-Cap (his real name has never been known) was a regular American until the Oklahoma City bombing, in which his girlfriend died. After that, he was desperate to sign up with the military to fight against terrorism. However, his psychiatric evaluation disqualified him for service.

Despite that, the Office of Naval Intelligence (ONI) offered him the opportunity to become a subject in the Navy's version of the Super-Soldier program. He leapt at the chance.

The ONI scientists grafted a neural net processor—a computer capable of learning—to Anti-Cap's spine. Its job was to control the dosage of the Super-Soldier drug acetovaxidol (known as AVX) administered to Anti-Cap. It was the same drug that had given powers to Cap's friend and Super Hero, Luke Cage.

After years of experiments with the computer, the drug still wasn't working. The admiral in charge of the project— Jimmy Westbrook—was ready to pull the plug in the aftermath of the September 11 attacks, but the Anti-Cap insisted he be given another chance. Westbrook took a gamble and shot him in the head.

This trauma finally activated the drug in the Anti-Cap's system, and he instantly grew from a scrawny man into his top physical potential. Already unstable, the transformation unbalanced him even farther.

The Anti-Cap worked for over two years as a deep-cover special forces soldier in Afghanistan, Syria, and Iraq. It wasn't until he was put into a version of a Captain America costume that he finally cracked—and went rogue. In the Anti-Cap's mind, he hadn't betrayed his country. He was adhering to his principles rather than his orders, just like he expected the real Cap would have done. The Anti-Cap used patches of the AVX drug to sustain his powers. Captain America trailed the Anti-Cap to France. In a final confrontation, he was given the chance to surrender, but Anti-Cap threw himself under a train.

The Anti-Cap takes Falcon hostage—something the real Cap would never have done.

"You are a product of America's hope. I am the sum of America's fears." ANTI-CAP

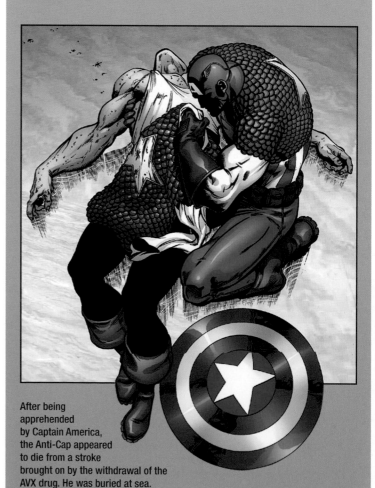

After being apprehended by Captain America, the Anti-Cap appeared to die from a stroke brought on by the withdrawal of the AVX drug. He was buried at sea.

The Anti-Cap's face looks nothing like Captain America's, though they have a similar build. Only with his mask on could he pass for Cap.

Anti-Cap's shield is similar in appearance to Cap's. However, it is not made out of the same unique materials (Vibranium and steel alloy) as the original.

The Anti-Cap chooses to carry various guns, knives, and explosives, which he is not afraid to use.

DATA FILE

FIRST APPEARANCE: *Captain America and the Falcon* #1 (May 2004)

REAL NAME: Unknown

AFFILIATIONS: Office of Naval Intelligence, US Navy SEALs, and US Marines.

POWERS AND ABILITIES: The Anti-Cap has superhuman durability, endurance, and strength, and has an accelerated healing factor. He is also an expert in unarmed combat and many kinds of weapons and firearms.

THE RETURN OF THE ANTI-CAP

Cap's Super Hero partner Falcon helped the Anti-Cap fake his death—thought to be from a stroke—so he could give him a chance to bring down Admiral Westbrook, who had made Falcon a fugitive from the law. The admiral had been secretly dealing with the Rivas drug gang, asking them to help him unlock the genetic secrets behind M.O.D.O.K. (Mental Organism Designed Only for Killing) and create a M.O.D.O.K. virus. When the conflict with Westbrook was over, Anti-Cap returned to hunting down the terrorists beyond the US military's reach. Cap tracked him down in Paris, France. Before he could bring him in, however, Anti-Cap jumped in front of a train.

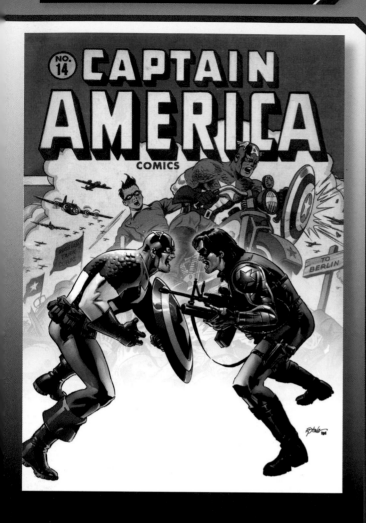

CAPTAIN AMERICA

VOL. 5 #14

"Remember! Remember who you really are!" CAPTAIN AMERICA

Main characters: Captain America; the Winter Soldier; Sharon Carter; Falcon **Supporting characters:** General Lukin; the Red Skull **Main locations:** Secret Base, mountains in West Virginia; Kronas Corporation Building; New York City; Fort Lehigh

April 2006

COVER ARTISTS
Alex Schomburg and Steve Epting

EDITORS
Tom Brevoort, Andy Schmidt, Molly Lazer, and Aubrey Sitterson

WRITER
Ed Brubaker

PENCILER, INKER
Steve Epting

LETTERER
Joe Caramagna

COLORIST
Frank D'Armata

BACKGROUND Writer Ed Brubaker's eight-year run on *Captain America* proved to be one of the most successful in the title's long history. It was filled with action-packed scenes and high-powered political intrigue—not to mention some of the greatest revelations in Cap's history. Brubaker's Marvel debut, *Captain America* Vol. 5 #1 (January 2005), began this new cycle with the death of an old villain, the Red Skull, at the hands of a mysterious Soviet assassin, known only as the Winter Soldier.

In comics, few things are considered sacred, but Bucky Barnes remaining dead had so far been one of them. It says a lot of Brubaker's talents—and Steve Epting's stunning visuals—that Bucky's return was not only embraced by readers, but his new alter ego, the Winter Soldier, became a fan favorite. Bucky's backstory had been revealed in the issues leading up to the tense conclusion of "The Winter Soldier" arc. At the end of World War II, the Russians had discovered his body and reprogrammed him to be their ultimate assassin. Stored in a form of suspended animation until needed, he had become a mythical figure throughout the world of espionage. A myth that Captain America was forced to confront in one of the most emotionally charged Cap stories of all time—and one that would prove to be a major turning point in Brubaker's epic run on the title.

THE STORY

Captain America has learned his old sidekick Bucky Barnes survived World War II and has been transformed into a deadly Soviet assassin. Now Cap must confront his friend and try to make him remember his past.

1

Rogue Russian general Aleksander Lukin had taken a Cosmic Cube from the Red Skull and recharged the device by letting off a WMD on American soil. His main operative was the Winter Soldier, a legendary Soviet assassin who Cap had learned was none other than a brainwashed Bucky Barnes. Concerned the Cube's power was too great, Lukin sent the Winter Soldier away with it.

Captain America and his allies managed to track the Cube to a secret base in the mountains west of Virginia, but the Winter Soldier was already waiting for them **(1)**. He was about to attack Falcon, only for the hero to be saved by a warning from his faithful bird, flying high above. Bucky retreated into the base, leaving Lukin's men to hold the gate. Cap followed him, as Falcon took on the guards. Sharon radioed Cap from her S.H.I.E.L.D. plane to inform him that she was still two minutes away with reinforcements, telling him that the base was a maze of tunnels—if the Winter Soldier managed to get clear, they would never find him. But the Winter Soldier was waiting for Cap. As their fight began **(2)**, Cap swore that he wouldn't fail Bucky again. Outside, Falcon defeated the first set of guards, only for more to blindside him. He was outnumbered and about to be shot when Sharon and a team of S.H.I.E.L.D. agents arrived in the nick of time, mowing down the rogue agents.

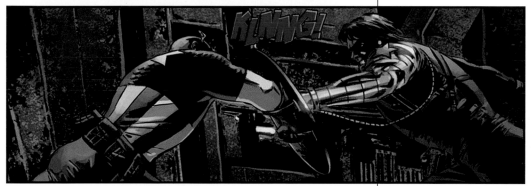

2

While Steve tried in vain to get through to his old friend, Bucky was holding nothing back in his efforts to kill Cap. In one last, desperate attempt, Cap dropped to his knees and told Bucky to go ahead and shoot if he truly didn't know who Cap was. Falcon and Sharon arrived on the scene just as Bucky pulled the trigger. Cap avoided the bullet and hurled his shield at his friend, knocking him over. The Cosmic Cube fell out of the Winter Soldier's backpack as he went down. Cap retrieved it and used its power to reverse Bucky's brainwashing.

3

Bucky's memories came flooding back **(3)**. He recalled everything, not just who he was, but all the things he'd done—both the good and the bad. The knowledge of what he had become seemed to break Bucky, who told Cap that he should've just killed him. Then Bucky snatched the Cube from Cap and seemed to destroy it with his cybernetic hand, its energy rushing out and enveloping him. When the energy melted away, there was no sign of either Bucky or the Cube. Sharon and Sam suspected that Bucky might have used the Cube to take his own life, but Cap told them they were wrong—Bucky was a survivor. Bucky was indeed alive, and had fled back to the place where it all began—Fort Lehigh army base **(4)**, where he had trained as Captain America's sidekick. Meanwhile, back in New York City, General Lukin was revealed to be sharing his mind with the consciousness of the Red Skull, both trapped in Lukin's mind like rats in a cage.

4

CAPTAIN AMERICA VOL. 6 #19
OCTOBER 2012

Steve Rogers once again tracked down William Burnside, the now-insane Cap of the 1950s. At Steve's request, S.H.I.E.L.D. faked William's death and gave him a new identity—along with treatment for his madness.
Cover art: Steve Epting

THE WINTER SOLDIER

When on the trail of a legendary assassin known as the Winter Soldier, Cap made a shocking discovery—it was Bucky, back from the dead.

Nick Fury and the global spy agency S.H.I.E.L.D. discovered intelligence about a notorious ex-Soviet killer called the Winter Soldier. He blended in perfectly with Americans, and he never seemed to age—because he was put into suspended animation between missions. He turned out to be Bucky Barnes, Captain America's former sidekick from their wartime days.

In modern times, under orders from ex-Russian General Aleksander Lukin, the Winter Soldier had killed Jack Monroe and had blown up part of Philadelphia, killing hundreds. He had assassinated the Red Skull and had stolen his Cosmic Cube, giving it to Lukin.

When the Cosmic Cube sent Cap a top-secret file on the Winter Soldier's past, Cap set out to track down his old friend. He cornered him in a secure facility in West Virginia, where the Winter Soldier had been sent to hide the Cube. Cap grabbed the Cube and used it to restore Bucky's memories. Distraught over his murderous actions, Bucky destroyed the Cube and vanished.

ORDERED TO KILL

As the Winter Soldier, Bucky traveled round the world, assassinating people on the orders of his Soviet masters. He was put back into suspended animation between missions. When he was sent to America, he disappeared for two weeks, wandering confused until his Soviet handlers found him. When his program shut down, he was left in a warehouse until Lukin reactivated him.

TAKE AIM...

Cap believed that there had to be some shred of Bucky left inside the Winter Soldier, but if that was true, that shred was buried very deep. Under orders from General Lukin to hide the Cosmic Cube in a secure facility and to kill anyone who came after it, the Winter Soldier had Captain America and the Falcon in his sights—and fired.

SOVIET ASSASSIN

When Baron Zemo's drone plane exploded back in 1945, supposedly killing both Bucky and Cap, a Soviet submarine rushed to the area and soon recovered Bucky's frozen body, which was missing its left arm. Soviet scientists revived him and gave him a bionic arm. With his memories lost, Bucky was brainwashed into being the perfect killer.

Captain America and the Winter Soldier engaged in hand-to-hand combat. Cap desperately wanted Bucky Barnes to remember who he really was deep down.

PAINFUL MEMORIES

Luckily, Cap was not hit and he grabbed the Cosmic Cube from the Winter Soldier and immediately used it, ordering Bucky to "Remember." The flood of memories that rushed into Bucky's head drove him to his knees. He not only remembered his childhood and his time working as Captain America's sidekick, but also the terrible crimes he had committed on behalf of his Russian masters.

IRON MAN

Billionaire industrialist and inventor Tony Stark created a suit of hi-tech powered armor that transforms him from a wealthy playboy into one of the most powerful Super Heroes in the world. As one of the founding Avengers, he has worked closely with Cap. Despite their friendship, the two have clashed on several occasions.

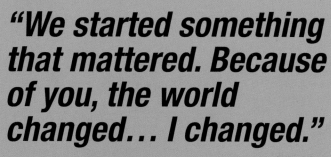

During the Superhuman Civil War, Cap and Iron Man found themselves leading opposing teams of heroes. Cap declared the Superhuman Registration Act unjust, while Tony chose to adhere to the law.

ORIGINS

The son of a wealthy inventor, Tony Stark assumed control of his father's company, Stark Industries, when he turned 21. Tony turned the engineering manufacturing company into a business that provided weapons for the US military.

While testing some of his latest inventions in Vietnam, Tony was injured by a bomb that embedded shrapnel near his heart. A warlord known as Wong-Chu captured Tony and set him working—along with fellow prisoner Ho Yinsen, a physicist—to create weapons for the Communists. Instead, Tony and Ho created a suit of powered armor that would not only allow Tony to escape, but would prevent the shrapnel from entering his heart. Tony freed his fellow prisoners and destroyed the prison camp before returning to the US where he used his suit to become the Super Hero known as Iron Man.

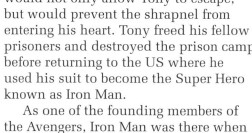

Iron Man's original suit was made from spare parts found at a prisoner-of-war camp.

As one of the founding members of the Avengers, Iron Man was there when Captain America was discovered in a block of ice. After Cap was thawed out, he joined the Avengers, and he and Tony became good friends. Together, they led the Avengers through many of their biggest challenges.

But the Super Heroes' friendship was called into question time after time. One of the most testing moments was during Iron Man's so-called "Armor Wars." Tony broke laws and betrayed friends in an attempt to destroy his technology, which had fallen into his business rival's hands. When Iron Man's crusade led him to break into a government installation, Cap was forced to lock Iron Man in the Vault prison. Later, the two disagreed over the Superhuman Registration Act—a law that required all Super Heroes to register with the US government. The law sparked a Superhuman Civil War, with Tony and Cap on opposite sides. They later reconciled to lead the Avengers again, but their relationship was never the same.

"We started something that mattered. Because of you, the world changed… I changed."

IRON MAN

With the imminent destruction of the multiverse, Cap declared Iron Man an enemy of the Avengers. He confronted Iron Man while wearing a suit of armor that Tony had designed.

Iron Man's armor includes the latest technology. Specially designed jet boots enable him to fly.

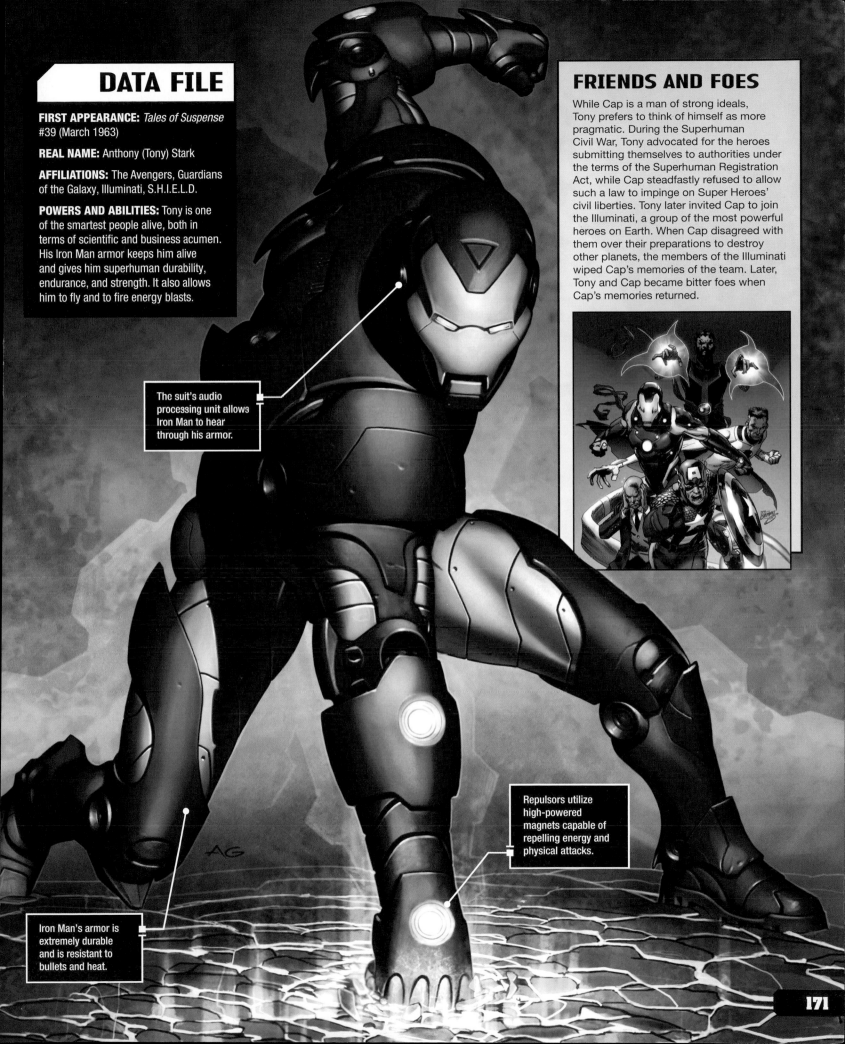

DATA FILE

FIRST APPEARANCE: *Tales of Suspense* #39 (March 1963)

REAL NAME: Anthony (Tony) Stark

AFFILIATIONS: The Avengers, Guardians of the Galaxy, Illuminati, S.H.I.E.L.D.

POWERS AND ABILITIES: Tony is one of the smartest people alive, both in terms of scientific and business acumen. His Iron Man armor keeps him alive and gives him superhuman durability, endurance, and strength. It also allows him to fly and to fire energy blasts.

The suit's audio processing unit allows Iron Man to hear through his armor.

Iron Man's armor is extremely durable and is resistant to bullets and heat.

Repulsors utilize high-powered magnets capable of repelling energy and physical attacks.

FRIENDS AND FOES

While Cap is a man of strong ideals, Tony prefers to think of himself as more pragmatic. During the Superhuman Civil War, Tony advocated for the heroes submitting themselves to authorities under the terms of the Superhuman Registration Act, while Cap steadfastly refused to allow such a law to impinge on Super Heroes' civil liberties. Tony later invited Cap to join the Illuminati, a group of the most powerful heroes on Earth. When Cap disagreed with them over their preparations to destroy other planets, the members of the Illuminati wiped Cap's memories of the team. Later, Tony and Cap became bitter foes when Cap's memories returned.

171

CIVIL WAR

What could cause the world's Super Hero community to turn on itself? The Civil War event saw Super Heroes split into warring factions with one side led by Iron Man and the other led by his former friend Captain America.

HERO VS. HERO

Super Heroes, from the X-Men to the Avengers, were no strangers to world-shaking events that forced them to team up against a greater threat. But the Civil War was the first crisis that pitted the heroes against themselves on purely philosophical grounds. The Superhuman Registration Act proposed that all Super Heroes unmask and reveal their true identities, and then undergo training to become licensed government employees. Iron Man was the first champion of the act, with Reed Richards of the Fantastic Four soon following suit. Captain America wasn't fond of Iron Man's "you're either with us or against us" attitude, and found himself heading up the opposition. As Cap led a team of Secret Avengers to help renegade heroes escape from government arrest squads, Iron Man oversaw the construction of a prison for dissidents. Spider-Man's defection from the pro-registration to the anti-registration side accelerated the need for Iron Man to force a battle royale between the two factions of the Civil War.

TRAGEDY IN STAMFORD

The Act came about following an incident where a team of inexperienced Super Heroes called the New Warriors tried to apprehend a quartet of costumed villains in the community of Stamford, Connecticut. A battle ensued and ended when the supercharged villain Nitro exploded, devastating the town and killing a group of children playing in a nearby park. Public outrage followed, with many people demanding that the government do something to prevent this happening again. Iron Man backed the Act, which would require all heroes to register with the government using their real names.

Iron Man and Cap discussed the disaster as Super Heroes helped the emergency services in the hunt for survivors. No one condoned the deaths of innocents in a reckless battle between heroes and villains, but Cap believed his old friend was using Stamford as an excuse to push through the Act. The danger, as Cap saw it, was that it would turn all Super Heroes into government lackeys.

The story continues...

KEY STORY

CAP GOES ROGUE

Captain America was one of the most prominent figures on the anti-registration side. He thought that this regulation was an example of the government overstepping its bounds, and explained his views to Maria Hill, the director of spy agency S.H.I.E.L.D. When she ordered Cap's arrest for failing to comply with the act, Cap broke free from a S.H.I.E.L.D. Helicarrier and became a wanted fugitive.

MIDNIGHT:

The news that each Super Hero had to register hit the headlines in response to the Stamford incident.

SECRET AVENGERS

Iron Man and his advisors—Reed Richards of the Fantastic Four and Hank Pym of the Avengers—made plans to deal with Cap's renegade status. Spider-Man joined them, famously unmasking himself on national television. Meanwhile, Cap's allies included Daredevil, Hercules, Luke Cage, and the Falcon. They carried out clandestine missions as the "Secret Avengers," helping the members of the Young Avengers escape from pro-registration capture squads.

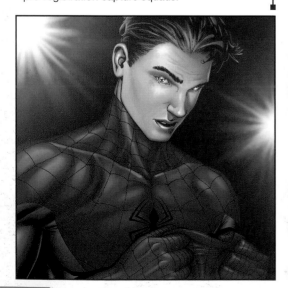

THE BATTLE IS ON

Iron Man's team faced off against Cap's team, hoping to defeat the opposition through sheer strength. Their secret weapon proved to be Thor—not the true God of Thunder, but a cloned cyborg duplicate. This Thor proved to be dangerously unstable. In a fight with Bill Foster—the size-changing hero known as Goliath—the Thor copy summoned lightning from the heavens, striking Goliath and killing him instantly. The shocking death of one of their own was too much for many on the pro-registration side. Spider-Man, the Invisible Woman, and the Human Torch switched allegiances and joined Captain America's team.

LAYING DOWN ARMS

A final battle was held to settle the Civil War.
Cap's team seemed outmatched, but the
tide turned when Namor's Atlantean warriors
made a surprise appearance and joined the
fight alongside the anti-registration outlaws.
But as the skirmish dragged on, Cap soon
realized that heroes should not be fighting
heroes—that they were only damaging their
reputation among those whom they were
meant to protect. A remorseful Cap turned
himself in to government custody. With the
Civil War over, the licensing of Super Heroes
began as Iron Man helped roll out the Fifty-
State Initiative—with each state having a
S.H.I.E.L.D.-sponsored Super Hero team.

175

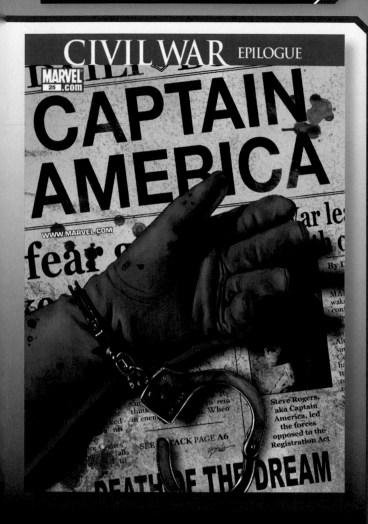

CIVIL WAR EPILOGUE

MARVEL .com 25

CAPTAIN AMERICA

WWW.MARVEL.COM

fear

Steve Rogers, aka Captain America, led the forces opposed to the Registration Act

SEE PACK PAGE A6

DEATH OF THE DREAM

April 2007

COVER ARTIST
Steve Epting

EDITORS
Tom Brevoort, Molly Lazer,
and Aubrey Sitterson

WRITER
Ed Brubaker

PENCILER, INKER
Steve Epting

LETTERER
Joe Caramagna

COLORIST
Frank D'Armata

CAPTAIN AMERICA

VOL. 5 #25

> "Captain America was pronounced dead on arrival." NEWSREADER

Main characters: Captain America; Bucky Barnes; Sharon Carter; Falcon; Crossbones **Supporting characters:** Doctor Faustus; General Lukin; Sin; the Red Skull **Main locations:** Federal Courthouse; Mercy Hospital; Manhattan

BACKGROUND While deaths of major comic characters have become semi-regular events, some of them still have quite an impact—none more so than the death of Captain America in 2007. An epilogue to the company-wide *Civil War* series, it proved to be one of the most explosive episodes of writer Ed Brubaker's award-winning run on the title. *Civil War* had seen Captain America not only fight his old Avengers ally Iron Man, but also turn against his own government and its laws, when he opposed the Superhuman Registration Act. With Iron Man's political views moving steadily more to the right, Cap represented an alternative viewpoint. Cap's forces had won the final battle of the Civil War, but Cap himself had surrendered when he saw the destruction it had caused. He realized that the public had turned against them. The saga reflected US tensions following 9/11 and drew on a broader worldwide discussion about governmental power versus individual liberty.

Captain America #25 was the month's best-selling title, with Cap going to trial—only to be assassinated on the steps of the courthouse. The story saw the Red Skull seize the opportunity presented by Cap's fall from grace to arrange his assassination. Cap's demise struck a chord in the tense political atmosphere of the time—it even got a real-world mention on ABC network news in the US. It had major repercussions across the entire Marvel line, too. A companion title, *Captain America: Fallen Son*, revealed how other Super Heroes dealt with the news. This issue marked the start of a new era, one that would eventually see Bucky Barnes take over Steve Rogers' uniform and become the next Captain America.

THE STORY

Captain America faces trial following the Superhuman Civil War. With many Americans now turned against him, Cap's allies are on guard as he is taken to court, but their worst fears are realized when an assassin strikes.

In the aftermath of the Superhuman Civil War, Captain America's arrest was a major news story. Reporters awaited his arrival for trial at Manhattan's Federal Courthouse, while crowds gathered—some supporting Cap, but many more calling him a traitor. Sharon Carter was among the onlookers, working with Nick Fury, Bucky Barnes, and the Falcon to try and protect Steve Rogers. She recalled how she had first seen Captain America in the old wartime newsreels her Aunt Peggy used to watch **(1)**. It was only later that she had realized her aunt had been in love with Captain America. Sharon had first met Cap early in her career with S.H.I.E.L.D., and had later fallen in love with him herself.

1

Bucky Barnes could only watch helplessly as his old friend arrived in a heavily armed convoy, surrounded by US Marshals **(2)**. He couldn't believe they planned to treat Captain America like some cheap criminal. The authorities wanted to crucify someone to appease the public, and so they had conveniently forgotten all the good Captain America had done for the country in World War II and since his return.

As Cap arrived at the courthouse, with the crowd yelling abuse, he noticed the red spot of a sniper's targeting laser on the back of one of the Marshals. Watching via hidden cameras, General Lukin revealed that he had used his influence to make sure Cap was transferred from S.H.I.E.L.D. custody in precisely this way. Back at the courthouse, Cap alerted the Marshal and quickly put himself between the marshal and the sniper's bullet. As Cap went down, one of the Marshals shouted "Sniper!" Panic ensued, as the horde of spectators tried to flee the scene. Sharon made her way through the terrified crowd toward Cap. Another shot was heard. Steve was down, with Sharon cradling his body **(3)**.

As Bucky searched for the sniper, he was confronted by Falcon, who at first believed Bucky to be the assassin. Bucky convinced him otherwise and, thanks to info from Nick Fury, learned the identity of the chief suspect. As Cap was rushed to the hospital, Bucky and Falcon teamed up to track down the sniper—Crossbones—finding him as he tried to escape in a helicopter. Bucky launched himself at the helicopter, bringing it down and subduing Crossbones after a brutal fight. He left him in Falcon's custody until S.H.I.E.L.D. agents arrived.

2

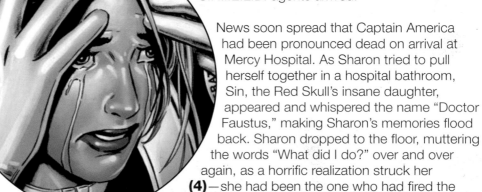

4

News soon spread that Captain America had been pronounced dead on arrival at Mercy Hospital. As Sharon tried to pull herself together in a hospital bathroom, Sin, the Red Skull's insane daughter, appeared and whispered the name "Doctor Faustus," making Sharon's memories flood back. Sharon dropped to the floor, muttering the words "What did I do?" over and over again, as a horrific realization struck her **(4)**—she had been the one who had fired the second shot. She had killed Captain America.

3

THE BURDEN OF DREAMS

Steve Rogers had been killed, but Captain America had to live on. Although unsure that he could fill his old friend's boots, Bucky Barnes still agreed to be the next Cap.

In pursuit of Captain America's killers, Bucky wound up captured by the villainous Red Skull. Austrian psychiatrist Doctor Faustus—who was working for the Skull—tried to reprogram him to become the ruthless Winter Soldier once more, but Bucky resisted. Bucky escaped with the help of a brainwashed Sharon Carter, but Falcon captured him and handed him over to anti-terror group S.H.I.E.L.D.

While Bucky was in the custody of S.H.I.E.L.D., Tony Stark—aka Iron Man and the director of the organization at the time—showed him a letter from Steve, to be delivered in the event of his death. It asked Tony to take care of Bucky. To that end, Tony asked Bucky to become the next Cap.

Bucky accepted the mantle, but he insisted on wearing a new costume and operating independently from S.H.I.E.L.D. Fighting like Cap turned out to be the easiest part of the job. Living up to his ideals was the real challenge.

WINTER SOLDIER RETURNS?

While imprisoned by the Red Skull, Bucky was subjected to brainwashing by Doctor Faustus—who was working for the villain. The Red Skull wanted the psychiatrist to return Bucky to his murderous Winter Soldier personality. But Bucky's will—bolstered by honest memories of his past—proved too strong for Faustus to pervert.

BUCKY EXPELLED

Falcon and Black Widow discovered that Bucky and Sharon Carter were being held by Faustus. Aware of the intruders, the doctor fled with Sharon and Bucky on his escape jet, with Falcon in pursuit. Fighting her own brainwashing by Doctor Faustus, Sharon Carter opened the back hatch and threw Bucky out of it. When Falcon stopped to save the free-falling Bucky, Faustus's jet escaped, but at least Cap's former sidekick was now in safe hands.

CAP'S LAST REQUEST

Falcon had rescued the falling Bucky and took him to the S.H.I.E.L.D. helicarrier. When Bucky came round, Iron Man was there and wanted to talk to him, offering Bucky the chance to take Steve Rogers' place as Cap. Bucky agreed on the condition that he wouldn't answer to anyone but himself.

NEW CAP, NEW MISSION

On his first mission as Cap, Bucky worked with the Black Widow, whom he had helped train when she was a young Russian spy. Unlike Steve, Bucky was willing to shoot down enemies in combat. When he tried to calm a riot, though, he found he didn't have Steve's gift for oratory and was unable to persuade the crowd that he was the real Cap.

CAPTAIN AMERICA: REBORN

Steve Rogers turned out not to be dead. His mind had been set loose in time, and he had had to fight his way back to save America and those he loved.

When Sharon Carter—under the influence of psychiatrist Doctor Faustus—supposedly shot Captain America dead on the steps of the Federal Courthouse, she unwittingly used a special gun designed by evil sorcerer Doctor Doom. This weapon froze Cap at that moment in time so that the Red Skull could later retrieve him and take over his body.

Sharon managed to foil the villains' plans by damaging the device that was supposed to bring back Cap. This led to Cap becoming unstuck in time, reliving moments of his life over and over again. Working with Doom, the Red Skull was able to transfer his mind into Steve's body, but Steve fought him for control inside, while his friends—including Bucky as the new Cap—fought the Red Skull and his forces outside.

This climaxed in a massive battle in front of the Lincoln Memorial and the Reflecting Pool in Washington, DC. By the end of it, Steve Rogers—the original Cap—had returned and the Red Skull was defeated.

TIME PLATFORM

Sharon and Steve were linked by nanoparticles in her blood, which could draw Steve to her through time. Doctor Doom built a machine for the Red Skull and Arnim Zola to pull Steve's body out of the time stream, after which they planned to move the Red Skull's mind into it. Sharon broke free and damaged the time platform, but Doctor Doom later repaired it.

SLIPPING THROUGH TIME

Lost in time, Steve was drawn helplessly from event to event in his long and storied history. He could affect things if he tried hard enough, but he worried that doing so would alter history. He eventually had the Vision record a message to the Avengers and then program himself to forget it until the present day.

UNCLE SKULL

When the Red Skull's mind moved from his robot body into Steve's body, Steve's mind became trapped in an illusory world Arnim Zola had constructed there: a place in which the Skull had conquered America. Steve's mind broke free, confronting the mind of the Red Skull for control of Steve's body.

SKULL VS. BUCKY CAP

While occupying Steve's body, the Red Skull fought Bucky. Rather than shoot who he thought was his old friend, Bucky hesitated and the Red Skull used Cap's shield to sever Bucky's bionic arm at the wrist. To stop the Red Skull killing Bucky, Steve engaged in a mental struggle with the villain for control of his body. When the Skull realized Steve was ready to kill them both, he fled.

ROBOT SKULL

Steve regained control of his own body and the Red Skull transferred his mind back to his robot version. To prevent him escaping, Sharon Carter hit him with a growth ray, but it turned him into a giant robot. While Steve, Bucky and other Super Heroes kept the Red Skull giant robot busy, Sharon, the Vision, and Ant-Man commandeered the Red Skull's ship and fired its missiles to destroy the huge Red Skull robot.

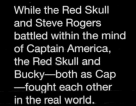

While the Red Skull and Steve Rogers battled within the mind of Captain America, the Red Skull and Bucky—both as Cap —fought each other in the real world.

SIEGE: CAPTAIN AMERICA #1
APRIL 2010

Steve Rogers and Bucky Barnes brought the united force of two Captain Americas to stand against Norman Osborn and his despotic plans to lay siege to Asgard. Cover art: Marko Djurdjevic

KEY STORY
FEAR ITSELF

The ancient Asgardian villain the Serpent, aka the God of Fear, made Earth a battleground for the gods, drawing Captain America into the fray.

Sin—now the new Red Skull—tracked down and claimed an enchanted hammer. As soon as she touched it, it transformed her into Skadi, the herald of the Serpent. Immediately she went to release the Serpent, aka the Asgardian God of Fear, from his prison beneath the ocean. The Serpent called seven more mystic hammers down to Earth. These possessed a number of other superhumans, transforming them into the Serpent's Worthy. Then he charged them to go and spread fear around Earth.

Thor was prophesied to fall in battle against the Serpent, nevertheless, he chose to stay with Cap and the Avengers to help them fight this threat. Meanwhile, Iron Man traveled to Asgard and used Odin's workshop to craft weapons for the team.

Odin, who turned out to be the Serpent's brother, was about to invade Earth in a bid to keep the God of Fear at bay. But just before his invasion, Odin's son Thor was able to slay the God of Fear, losing his own life, but saving Earth.

WAR MACHINES

As the rest of the Worthy were being chosen by their hammers—and possessed by their namesakes—Skadi set out to spread as much fear as she could in order to feed the Serpent's appetite. To that end, Skadi constructed giant Nazi mechs and turned her army against Washington, DC, destroying it.

SIN AS SKADI

The original Red Skull had called the hammer of Skadi to Earth, hoping to use its power, but he could not lift it. His daughter Sin learned about it in a dream in which she killed Cap with the hammer, and she tracked it down. She lifted it easily, and the hammer instantly transformed her into Skadi, the herald of the Serpent, Asgardian God of Fear.

BUCKY KILLED

Bucky (as Captain America), Black Widow, and Falcon battled Skadi and her Nazi war machines in Washington, DC. When Bucky faced down Skadi, though, her power proved too much. She tore off his bionic arm and then drove the handle of her hammer through him, along with a massive bolt of lightning, apparently killing him.

While battling the Serpent, Thor lost his hammer, Mjolnir, which could only be wielded by one found worthy of its power. Cap scooped it up, and shouting "Avengers Assemble!" led the Avengers into the fight.

CAP IS BACK

With Bucky dead, Steve Rogers realized that someone had to carry his old shield and fill his old boots. Steve donned his Captain America costume again and led the Avengers into battle against the forces of the God of Fear and his Worthy, Skadi.

SHATTERED SHIELD

When Cap faced off against the Serpent, he threw his shield at the God of Fear, who raised it above his head and shattered it with his bare hands. When Thor launched his final assault against the Serpent, he threw Mjolnir at him, but it bounced away. Thor used the Odinsword, aka Ragnarok, to finally slay the Serpent, but he also perished in the battle. Later, the smiths in Odin's workshop repaired the shield, but a battle scar remained.

AGE OF ULTRON #7
MAY 2013

When Hank Pym was killed to prevent the creation of Ultron—and save the world from him—a new timeline was created in which Colonel America led a different version of the Defenders—who were later destroyed by Morgan le Fay. Cover art: Brandon Peterson

KEY STORY

TRAPPED IN DIMENSION Z

Captured by Arnim Zola and brought to Dimension Z—an alternate reality discovered by Zola—Cap struggled to raise an infant boy and find his way back home.

Following a procedure that saw bioengineer Arnim Zola inject Captain America with a virus, Cap broke free and escaped with an infant he thought Arnim was experimenting on. The boy was Arnim's son whom Arnim was growing out of bio-gel. Lost in the wilds of Dimension Z, Cap raised the boy—calling him Ian—for 12 years.

Arnim and his daughter Jet Black recovered Ian and brainwashed him into joining them. Cap tried to rescue Ian, only to have the boy beat him nearly to death. As the boy held a gun to Cap's head, Cap asked him who he was: Leopold Zola or Ian Rogers?

The boy chose to remain as Ian, but unaware of this, S.H.I.E.L.D. agent Sharon Carter appeared and shot him. Sharon had placed explosives under Arnim's city and as Cap raced to escape Dimension Z, Sharon detonated the explosives, sacrificing herself to bring down Arnim Zola.

CAPTURED BY ZOLA

Arnim captured Cap to keep him from interfering with his plans to invade Earth. He injected him with a Zola virus that would allow his mind to take over Cap. Cap was able to snap his bonds and escape, taking Ian with him. Arnim thought Ian had been killed, and swore vengeance.

ZOLA'S PLANS EXPOSED

After finding a home for himself and young Ian with the natives of Dimension Z—creatures known as the Phrox—Cap was forced to fight with their tyrannical leader, Zofjor. During the battle, Zofjor slashed open Cap's chest, exposing the results of Arnim's Zola virus: it was apparent that Zola's consciousness had grown inside Cap's chest.

LIKE FATHER, LIKE SON

Cap raised Ian in the wastelands of Dimension Z for 12 years. Although Ian knew he had been adopted, he thought of Cap as his father. Not only did Cap teach Ian how to fight and survive in such a dangerous land, he also taught him compassion, love, and the importance of standing up for yourself.

WHAT'S IN A NAME?

After Arnim recovered Ian, he brainwashed the boy into becoming one of his most ardent followers. This included taking the name Leopold Zola and turning against Cap as the one who had stolen him from his real father. Arnim wanted the boy to kill Cap as a means of proving his loyalty to the Zola family.

For decades, Arnim Zola labored in the shadows, working mostly on behalf of the Red Skull. The discovery of Dimension Z and its much faster rate of time allowed him to finally set into place his own plans to both destroy Captain America and conquer the world.

SHARON'S SACRIFICE

Sharon had rigged Arnim's flying city with explosives, but she needed to be closer to detonate them. Despite only being seconds away from escaping Dimension Z with Cap and Jet Black, she slipped free from Cap's grasp. While standing on top of a gigantic version of Zola's body, she detonated the charges and brought down the whole city.

189

IAN ROGERS

Created by Arnim Zola to become the perfect son for his fiendish plans, Ian Rogers was instead rescued by Captain America from Zola's headquarters when he was still a baby. Young Ian grew up alongside the Super Hero, who treated him like his own son, but life for the boy in Dimension Z became increasingly complicated.

Not knowing who the infant Ian was, Cap decided to be like a father to him and protect him while they were living in Dimension Z.

ORIGINS

As part of his long-term plans, Arnim Zola decided to create the perfect children for himself, using his amazing bio-gel. His first was his daughter, Jet Black, and his second was a son, Ian. They were born in Dimension Z, a place dominated by Arnim, where time ran much faster than in the regular world.

When Ian was a baby, still growing in a liquid-filled tube, Arnim captured Captain America and brought him to Dimension Z. As Cap

escaped through a window, he grabbed the baby, taking him with him. Lost and stranded in the wilds of Dimension Z, Cap raised Ian on his own for 11 years, teaching him how to throw his shield, and the two grew close. Much of their time was spent alongside the native aliens known as the Phrox.

When Arnim discovered his son was still alive, he and Jet reclaimed the boy. Arnim set to brainwashing Ian into loving him and becoming the son he'd always intended him to be: a vicious, cold, and heartless child known as Leopold Zola. He then urged the boy

Cap was relieved to find that the baby he'd rescued from Arnim's lab was unharmed.

to kill Cap, who had come to claim him. When faced with the opportunity to end Cap's life, though, the boy couldn't manage it. Instead, he declared his name was Ian Rogers.

At the same time, overwhelmed by the fact her brother was still alive, and stunned by his compassion, Jet began to question everything her father had taught her. She turned against Zola, hoping to escape Dimension Z with her brother Ian at her side. Before anyone could get Ian out of Dimension Z, however, S.H.I.E.L.D. agent Sharon Carter found them.

Mistakenly thinking Ian was going to kill Cap, Sharon shot the boy through the neck. He fell into a gigantic pit of bio-gel, and sank without a trace. Ian had originally been created using bio-gel, so the compound healed the boy, thus saving his life. However, Cap had already departed from Dimension Z, still believing that his adopted son had perished.

"I always stand up. Like my dad taught me." IAN ROGERS

After Cap escaped from Dimension Z, thinking his son to be dead, Ian continued the fight against his father, Arnim Zola. He came to be called Nomad by the native species.

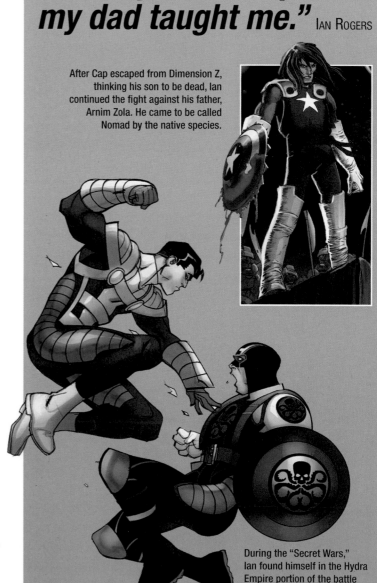

During the "Secret Wars," Ian found himself in the Hydra Empire portion of the battle arena planet, Battleworld. There, he fought an alternate version of himself, Leopold Zola.

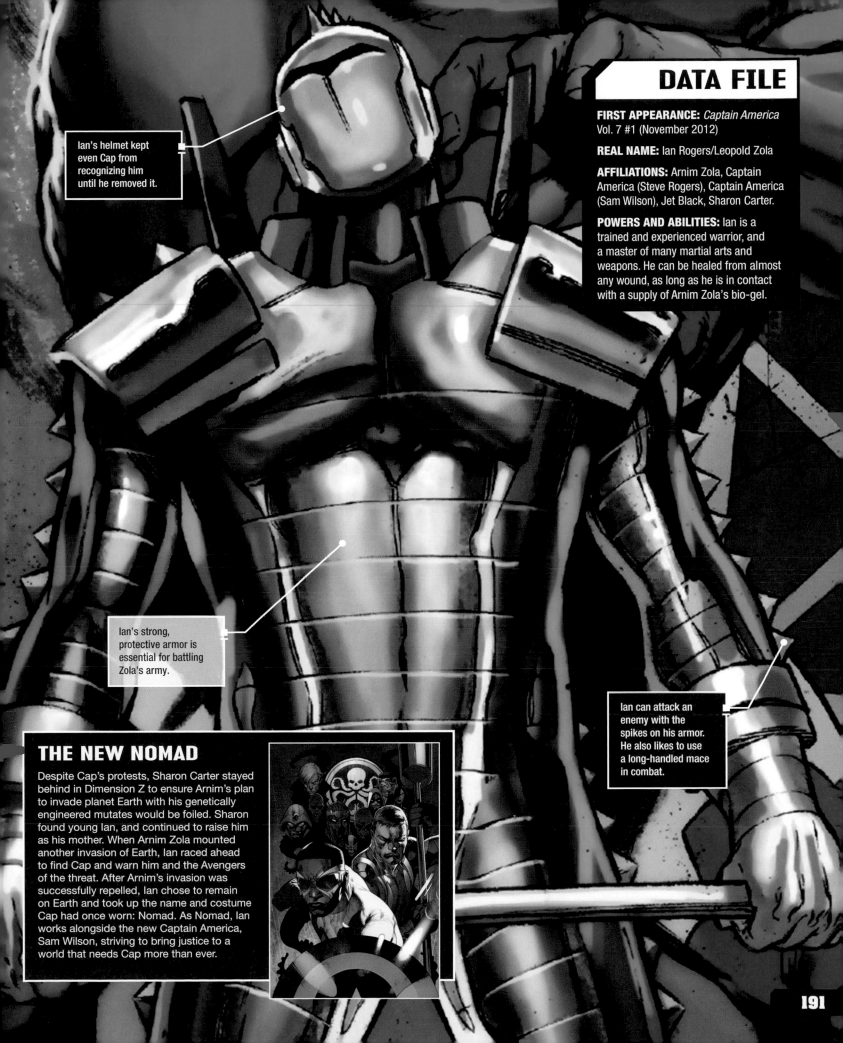

Ian's helmet kept even Cap from recognizing him until he removed it.

DATA FILE

FIRST APPEARANCE: *Captain America* Vol. 7 #1 (November 2012)

REAL NAME: Ian Rogers/Leopold Zola

AFFILIATIONS: Arnim Zola, Captain America (Steve Rogers), Captain America (Sam Wilson), Jet Black, Sharon Carter.

POWERS AND ABILITIES: Ian is a trained and experienced warrior, and a master of many martial arts and weapons. He can be healed from almost any wound, as long as he is in contact with a supply of Arnim Zola's bio-gel.

Ian's strong, protective armor is essential for battling Zola's army.

Ian can attack an enemy with the spikes on his armor. He also likes to use a long-handled mace in combat.

THE NEW NOMAD

Despite Cap's protests, Sharon Carter stayed behind in Dimension Z to ensure Arnim's plan to invade planet Earth with his genetically engineered mutates would be foiled. Sharon found young Ian, and continued to raise him as his mother. When Arnim Zola mounted another invasion of Earth, Ian raced ahead to find Cap and warn him and the Avengers of the threat. After Arnim's invasion was successfully repelled, Ian chose to remain on Earth and took up the name and costume Cap had once worn: Nomad. As Nomad, Ian works alongside the new Captain America, Sam Wilson, striving to bring justice to a world that needs Cap more than ever.

INVASION OF ZOLA

Arnim Zola survived Sharon Carter's attempt to destroy him and his city. With time working so much faster in Dimension Z, he was able to rebuild his city and his mutates in relatively little time. He was able to attack Manhattan by opening a portal from Dimension Z into Central Park.

IAN REVEALS HIMSELF

After the mysterious warrior from Dimension Z fought his way past Iron Man, Thor, and the Hulk, Steve took him down. The man then stood up and removed his helmet, revealing that he was Ian Rogers, all grown up. He had not come to attack but to warn Steve and the rest of the Avengers about Zola's invasion.

THE TOMORROW SOLDIER

After the Super-Soldier serum was drained from Steve Rogers, he aged rapidly into an old man. Now someone younger had to carry on Cap's legacy.

As an aged Steve rested in Avengers Mansion, evil bio-geneticist Arnim Zola launched an invasion on New York City from the alternate reality Dimension Z. A lone man raced ahead to warn the Super Heroes. He was Ian Rogers, Arnim's son, now an adult.

The Avengers fought Arnim's army which included twisted versions of themselves called the Unvengers. Meanwhile, Cap's partner Falcon and Arnim's daughter Jet Black—who had turned against her father when she had discovered his villainy—entered Arnim's headquarters that had appeared through a portal in Central Park. They found that spy agency S.H.I.E.L.D. operative Sharon Carter was alive. The Avengers confronted Arnim and drew him out into the streets of Manhattan while Ian rescued Sharon. The heroes discovered that Arnim had a bomb to blow up the city. To save everyone, Falcon grabbed the bomb and flew it high into the sky where it detonated. Fortunately, he was unharmed. Later, Steve announced that the Falcon would succeed him as the new Captain America.

RETURN OF SHARON CARTER

Falcon and Jet Black—who had recently started a relationship—flew to Central Park to help fight Arnim's invaders. They entered Arnim's headquarters and discovered Sharon Carter, who was being held prisoner. She had survived the explosion of Arnim's previous city, after which she had found Ian and raised him, becoming his adoptive mother.

FOR THE LOVE OF JET

When Jet confronted her father, Arnim told her that her betrayal of him had all been part of his master plan. Arnim urged her to rejoin him, but Falcon intervened, dragging Arnim out of his headquarters and into the streets of Manhattan. The two men fought not only over the fate of the city, but also over Jet.

A week after Falcon's heroic action to save New York City from Arnim's bomb, Steve called the Avengers together to announce that he could no longer continue as Captain America. He and Sharon would lead the Avengers as their mission operators. However, he was passing on the shield to the Falcon—Sam Wilson—who would now be the new Captain America.

SECRET WARS #0
JUNE 2015

The multiverse collapsed during the Secret Wars, leaving only a single universe—known as Battleworld—ruled over by Doctor Doom. Steve Rogers died while battling Iron Man in their universe's final moments.
Cover art: Alex Ross

INDEX

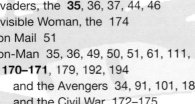